Workshop on Automatic Text Simplification Methods and Applications in the Multilingual Society 2014

Held at COLING 2014

Dublin, Ireland
24 August 2014

ISBN: 978-1-63439-224-2

Printed from e-media with permission by:

Curran Associates, Inc.
57 Morehouse Lane
Red Hook, NY 12571

Printed by Curran Associates, Inc. (2014)

For permission requests, please contact the Association for Computational Linguistics at the address below.

Association for Computational Linguistics
209 N. Eighth Street
Stroudsburg, Pennsylvania 18360

Phone: 1-570-476-8006
Fax: 1-570-476-0860

acl@aclweb.org

Additional copies of this publication are available from:

Curran Associates, Inc.
57 Morehouse Lane
Red Hook, NY 12571 USA
Phone: 845-758-0400
Fax: 845-758-2634
Email: curran@proceedings.com
Web: www.proceedings.com

Introduction

The remarkable development of language technology tools in recent years in terms of robustness, computational speed and volume of processed data, together with the increasing number of languages covered, made possible their usage not only for specific research applications, but also for real world applications which prove useful in everyday life. Automatic correction of text, machine translation, extraction of important information and interaction with devices using speech are just some of these applications. Language technology now has the maturity to be used for addressing societal challenges such as helping people with disabilities, the elderly and migrants.

However, due to the ambiguity and complexity of natural language, its automatic processing is still very challenging and benefits from processing shorter and less ambiguous information. The same is true for people who have difficulties understanding text due to disabilities, or who have to read texts in a language they do not have a good command of. In all these cases, automatic text simplification can prove to be very useful.

In contrast to controlled languages, which practically create a sublanguage by imposing constraints on the grammar rules, discourse style, number of words in a sentence etc., text simplification eliminates or replaces parts of sentences or paragraphs, or even reformulates them according to specific requirements of the target user groups. Among the most frequent techniques are: lexical substitution, verb forms replacement (for morphologically rich languages), word order adjustments, deletion of subordinate clauses, replacement of anaphoric pronouns by their reference, usage of synonym expressions with higher frequency as well as compound splitting.

This workshop intends to bring together scientists working in a variety of fields in which text simplification can be applied, computational linguists interested in the research problems of text simplification and of course users who can benefit from the simplified texts.

The innovative aspect of this workshop is its focus on text simplification from two perspectives: On the one hand, how computational linguistics applications which simplify texts can be used by people in real world situation, and on the other hand, how to simplify the input for other NLP-based applications in order to improve their accuracy.

We are happy we could include in the workshop programme contributions dealing with all aforementioned issues.

Iustin Dornescu, Richard Evans and Constantin Orăsan report in *Relative clause extraction for syntactic simplification* about their results on syntactic text simplification method which focuses on extracting embedded clauses from structurally complex sentences and rephrasing them without affecting the original meaning.

In the paper *Making Biographical Data in Wikipedia Readable: A Pattern-based Multilingual Approach* the authors (Itziar Gonzalez-Dios, María Jesús Aranzabe and Arantza Díaz de Ilarraza) present Biographix a tool meant to create simple readable and accessible sentences in Wikipedia articles related to biographies. The tools is originally designed for Basque and then adapted for five European languages.

The contribution *Exploring the effects of Sentence Simplification on Hindi to English Machine Translation System* by Kshitij Mishra, Ankush Soni, Rahul Sharma and Dipti Sharma shows how text simplification can be used for bringing forward research in Machine Translation.

Ruslav Mitkov and Sanja Štajner introduce in their paper *The Fewer the better? A Contrastive Study about Ways to Simplify* a minimal set of rules which ensure a readability close to that one obtained by applying a long list of more fine-grained rules.

In *Automatic Text Simplification For Handling Intellectual Property (The Case of Multiple Patent Claims)* Svetlana Sheremetyeva presents an on-going project on a multi-level text simplification to assist experts who work on handling intellectural property in patent claims.

A User-View on adequate language resources to be used for txt simplifications is presented in the paper *Assessing Conformance of Manually Simplified Corpora with User Requirements: the Case of Autistic Readers* by Sanja Štajner, Richard Evans and Iustin Dornescu

In *Making historical Texts accessible for the crowd*, the authors explain which kind of simplification and adaptation historical texts may go through in order to be accessible to researchers and broad public not familiar with languages of previous centuries.

We hope that the workshop will contribute to the development of a roadmap of activities, tools and resources on text simplification from a multilingual perspective, roadmap which we think to be absolutely necessary for ensuring advances in this intriguing research field.

The organising committee would like to thank to the Programme Committee which contributed with very fast but substantial reviews to the workshop programme

Constantin Orăsan, Petya Osenova and Cristina Vertan

Organizers:

Constantin Orăsan, University of Wolverhampton, UK

Petya Osenova, Sofia University "St. Kl. Ohridski", Bulgaria

Cristina Vertan, University of Hamburg, Germany

Program Committee:

Eric Atwell, Leeds University, UK
Eduard Barbu, University of Jaen, Spain
Ann Copestake, University of Cambridge, UK
Iustin Dornescu, University of Wolverhampton, UK
Richard Evans, University of Wolverhampton, UK
Thomas François, University of Louvain, Belgium
David Gil, Deletrea, Spain
Vesna Jordanova, Imperial College London, UK
Walther v. Hahn, University of Hamburg, Germany
Veronique Hoste, University College Gent, Belgium
Elena Lloret, University of Alicante, Spain
Annie Louis, University of Edinburgh, UK
Maite Martin Valdivia, University of Jaen, Spain
Paloma Moreda, University of Alicante, Spain
Hitoshi Nishikawa, NTT, Japan
Maciej Ogrodniczuk, Polish Academy of Sciences, Poland
Pavel Pecina, Charles University Prague, Czech Republic
Gabor Proszeky, Morphologic, Hungary
Horacio Saggion, Universitat Pompeu Fabra, Spain
Advaith Siddharthan, University of Aberdeen, UK
Lucia Specia, Sheffield University, UK
Sara Tonelli, FBK, Italy
Hristo Tanev, JRC, Italy
Dan Tufis, Romanian Academy, Romania
Dusko Vitas, University of Belgrade, Serbia

Invited Speaker:

Advaith Siddharthan, University of Aberdeen, UK

Table of Contents

The Fewer, the Better? A Contrastive Study about Ways to Simplify

Ruslan Mitkov and **Sanja Štajner**
Research Group in Computational Linguistics
Research Institute of Information and Language Processing
University of Wolverhampton, UK
{R.Mitkov, SanjaStajner}@wlv.ac.uk

Abstract

Simplified texts play an important role in providing accessible and easy-to-understand information for a whole range of users who, due to linguistic, developmental or social barriers, would have difficulty in understanding materials which are not adapted and/or simplified. However, the production of simplified texts can be a time-consuming and labour-intensive task. In this paper we show that the employment of a short list of simple simplification rules could result in texts of comparable readability to those written as a result of applying a long list of more fine-grained rules. We also prove that the simplification process based on the short list of simple rules is more time efficient and consistent.

1 Rationale

Simplified texts play an important role in providing accessible and easy-to-understand information for a whole range of users who, due to linguistic, developmental or social barriers, would have difficulty in understanding materials which are not adapted and/or simplified. Such users include but are not limited to people with insufficient knowledge of the language in which the document is written, people with specific language disorders and people with low literacy levels. However, while the production of simplified texts is certainly an indispensable activity, it often proves to be a time-consuming and labour-intensive task. Various methodologies and simplification strategies have been developed which are often employed by authors to simplify original texts. Most methods involve a high number of rules which could result not only in the simplification task being time-consuming but also in the authors getting confused as to which rules to apply. We hypothesise that it is possible to achieve a comparable simplification effect by using a small set of simple rules similar to the ones used in Controlled Languages which, in addition, enhances the productivity and reliability of the simplification process.

In order to test our hypothesis we conduct the following experiments. First, we propose six Controlled Language-inspired rules which we believe are simple and easy enough for writers of simplified texts to understand and apply. We then ask two writers to apply these rules to a selection of newswire texts and also to produce simplified versions of these texts using the 28 rules used in the Simplext project (Saggion et al., 2011). Both sets of texts are compared in terms of readability. In both simplification tasks the time efficiency is assessed and the inter-annotator agreement is evaluated. In an additional experiment, we seek to investigate the possible effect of familiarisation in simplification. In this experiment a third writer simplifies a sample of the texts used in the previous experiments by applying each set of rules in a mixed sequence pattern which does not offer any familiarisation nor the advantage of one set of rules over the other. Using these samples, three-way inter-annotator agreement is reported.

The rest of the paper is structured as follows. Section 2 outlines related work on simplification rules. Section 3 introduces our proposal for a small set of easy-to-understand and easy-to-apply rules and contrasts them with the longer and more elaborate rules employed in the Simplext proposal. Section 4 details the experiments conducted in order to validate or refute our hypothesis, and outlines the data used for the experiments. Section 5 presents and discusses the results, while the last section of the paper summarises the main conclusions of this study.

2 Related work

Since the late 1990s, several initiatives which proposed guidelines for producing plain, easy-to-read and more accessible documents have emerged. These include the "Federal Plain Language Guidelines", "Make it Simple, European Guidelines for the Production of Easy-to-Read Information for people with Learning Disability", and "Am I making myself clear? Mencap's guidelines for accessible writing".

The Plain Language Action and Information Network (PLAIN)[1] developed the first version of the "Federal Plain Language Guidelines" (PlainLanguage, 2011) in the mid-90s and have revised it every few years since then. Their original idea was to help writers of governmental documents (primarily regulations) to write in a clear and and simple manner so that the users can: "find what they need; understand what they find; and use what they find to meet their needs." (PlainLanguage, 2011). The "Make it Simple" European Guidelines for the Production of Easy-to-Read Information for people with Learning Disability (Freyhoff et al., 1998) were produced by Inclusion Europe[2] in order to assist writers in developing texts, publications and videos that are more accessible to people with intellectual disabilities and other people who cannot read complex texts, and thus enable those people to be better protected from discrimination and social injustice. The "Am I making myself clear?" Mencap's guidelines for accessible writing (Mencap, 2002) were produced by the UK's leading organisation working with people with a learning disability.[3] Their goal is to help in editing and writing accessible material for that specific target population. All of these guidelines are concerned with both verbal content of documents and their layout. As we are interested in text simplification and not in text representation, we will concentrate only on the former. All three guidelines share similar instructions for accessible writing, some of them more detailed than others. Table 1 allows us to have a quick overview of intersecting rules suggested by these guidelines which were intended for slightly different purposes and target audiences.. For example, they all advise the writer to use active voice instead of passive, use short, simple words and omit unnecessary words, write short sentences and cover only one main idea per sentence, etc. However, the "Federal Plain Language Guidelines" also instruct writers to use contractions where appropriate, avoid hidden verbs (i.e. verbs converted into a noun), and place the main idea before exceptions and conditions, while the other two guidelines do not go into many details. Some of the instructions, e.g. to use the simplest form of a verb (present and not conditional or future), or to avoid double negatives and exceptions to exceptions, are not present in the Mencap's guidelines for accessible writing, while they are at the same time implicitly present in the "Make it Simple" guidelines, and explicitly present in the "Federal Plain Language Guidelines".

Karreman et al. (2007) investigated whether the application of the "Make it Simple" guidelines to the website's content would enhance its usability for users with intellectual disabilities. Additionally, they investigated whether the application of these guidelines would have a negative effect on users without disabilities, as Web Accessibility Initiative (WAI) guidelines[4] state that creation of multiple versions of the same website should be avoided whenever possible. The authors prepared two versions of a website, the original one and the one adapted according to the "Make it Simple" guidelines. These two versions were then tested for efficiency (searching and reading time) and effectiveness (comprehension) by 40 participants, 20 with diagnosed intellectual disabilities and 20 without. The results demonstrated that the adaptation of the website according to the guidelines enhanced the efficiency and effectiveness for both groups of participants.

There has been a body of work associated with the development and use of Controlled Languages for simplification purposes. The original idea of developing a Controlled Language arose during the 1930s when influential scholars sought to establish a 'minimal' variety of English, a variety specifically designed to make English accessible to and usable by the largest possible number of people worldwide (Arnold et al., 1994). This variety was called Basic English and one of the central ideas was to use a few hundred general-purpose words only. Operator verbs were to be used with a set of nouns and

[1]http://www.plainlanguage.gov/

[2]http://inclusion-europe.org/

[3]http://november5th.net/resources/Mencap/Making-Myself-Clear.pdf

[4]http://www.w3.org/WAI/

Rule	Simple	Clear	Plain
Use active tense (instead of passive)	yes	yes	yes
Use the simplest form of a verb*	(yes)		yes
Avoid hidden verbs (i.e. verbs converted into a noun)			yes
Use 'must' to indicate requirements			yes
Use contractions where appropriate			yes
Don't turn verbs into nouns			yes
Use 'you' to speak directly to readers	yes	yes	yes
Avoid abbreviations	yes		yes
Use short, simple words	yes		yes
Omit unnecessary words			yes
Avoid definitions as much as possible			yes
Use the same term consistently		yes	yes
Avoid legal, foreign and technical jargon	yes	yes	yes
Don't use slashes			yes
Write short sentences	yes	yes	yes
Keep subject, verb and object close together			yes
Avoid double negatives and exceptions to exceptions	(yes)		yes
Place the main idea before exceptions and conditions			yes
Cover only one main idea per sentence	yes	yes	
Use examples (avoid abstract concepts)	yes		yes
Keep the punctuation simple	yes	yes	
Be careful with figures of speech and metaphors	yes		
Use the number and not the word	yes	yes	
Avoid cross references	yes		yes

*Use present tense and not conditional or future

Table 1: Rules for verbal content of documents (the three columns 'Simple', 'Clear', and 'Plain' contain 'yes' if this rule is present in the corresponding guidelines: "Make it Simple", "Am I making myself clear?" and "Federal Plain Language Guidelines", respectively; value '(yes)' is used when the rule is not explicitly present in the corresponding guidelines, only implicitly)

adjectives to replace most of the derived verbs. The Controlled Language writing rules included various rules such as 'Keep it short and simple' (Keep sentences short, Omit redundant words, Order the parts of the sentence logically, Don't change constructions in mid-sentence, Take care with the logic of and and or) and 'Make it explicit' (Avoid elliptical constructions, Don't omit conjunctions or relatives, Adhere to the PACE dictionary, Avoid strings of nouns, Do not use -ing unless the word appears thus in the PACE dictionary) (Arnold et al., 1994). The concept of controlled languages evolved and developed further and they have been regarded as a prerequisite part of successful Machine Translation. Controlled Languages have been also employed in a number of critical situations where ambiguity could be a problem.[5]

3 Simplification strategies: contrasting two sets of rules

The Simplext guidelines were written under the Simplext project, with the aim of helping the authors to produce texts which would be accessible to people with Down syndrome. They follow the same main ideas as those in "Make it Simple, European Guidelines for People with Intellectual Disability" but they adapt the rules to their specific target population and the Spanish language. The Simplext guidelines contain 28 main rules[6] concerned with the verbal content of documents. Those rules cover the same main ideas as our rules (see below), e.g. to keep sentences short, use only the most frequent words,

[5]The reader is referred to (Kittredge, 2003), (Cardey, 2009) and (Temnikova, 2012) for more details.

[6]The Simplext guidelines actually provide even more sub-rules for most of the main rules, but in this study we use only the 28 main rules.

remove redundant words, use a simpler paraphrase if applicable. However, the Simplext rules are more fine-grained, thus providing several more specific rules instead of our more general rules. For example, they explicitly instruct the writer to use frequent words, use non-ambiguous words, and not use words with more than six syllables whenever it is possible.

On the other hand, the six simple rules selected for our study have been inspired from the rules in Controlled Languages[7]. We conjecture that there is a small set of simple, easy-to-understand and easy-to-apply rules which can be equally efficient in terms of simplicity (readability) and yet their employment is less time-consuming and less contentious in practice. The rules which we propose are as follows (examples are presented in Table 2):

1. **Use simple sentences**

   We have selected this rule to ensure that the simplified version of the document features sufficiently short and simple sentences only so that the reader does not have to process longer complex sentences.

2. **Remove anaphors**

   This rules caters for replacing the anaphors such as pronouns and one-anaphors with their antecedent to minimise the risk of anaphoric ambiguity but also makes sure that the texts does not feature any elliptical constructions which may be more difficult to understand.

3. **Use active voice only**

   We have included this rule as active voice is generally easier to process.

4. **Use the most frequent words only**

   Similarly to the practice recommended in Basic English, we recommend the use of the 1,000 most frequent words in Spanish as documented by RAE (Real Academia Española)[8]. If this is not possible, then words from the list of the 5,000 most frequent Spanish words are resorted to[9]. We have allowed the following exception for this rule. There are cases where a specific technical word occurs in the text and which is unlikely to be on the list of 1,000 (or 5,000) basic / most frequent words in Spanish. By way of example, in the sentence 'Ana Juan ganó el Premio Nacional de Ilustración de 2010' (Ana Juan won the national prize for illustration in 2010) the word *Ilustración* is considered as technical and is not replaced with a basic word.

5. **Remove redundant words**

   Our rules recommend the removal of redundant words or phrases which do not really contribute to the understanding of the text.

6. **Use a simpler paraphrase, if applicable**

   There are cases where the sentence is difficult to read or understand due among other things, to its syntax. Our rules recommend that in such cases the original sentence or part of the sentence is paraphrased.

4 Experiments and data

In order to test our hypothesis we conducted several experiments. We selected 10 newswire texts in Spanish and asked two writers who are native speakers of Spanish and who have a language/linguistics background, to apply both our six rules and the 28 Simplext rules in order to simplify these newswire texts. The writers familiarised themselves with the rules beforehand, had an induction with the authors

[7]We shall often refer to these rules throughout the paper as 'our rules'

[8]http://corpus.rae.es/frec/1000_formas.TXT

[9]http://corpus.rae.es/frec/5000_formas.TXT

Rule	Version	Example
1	Original	Desde hace ya 10 años, La Casa Encendida ha propuesto y desarrollado, dentro del mundo profesional de las Artes Escénicas, el Ciclo Artes Escénicas y Discapacidad. [*It is now 10 years ago that La Casa Encendida first proposed and carried out, within the professional field of performing arts, the performing arts and disabilities course.*]
	Simplified	Desde hace ya 10 años, La Casa Encendida ha organizado el Ciclo Artes Escénicas y Discapacidad**. El** Ciclo Artes Escénicas y Discapacidad está dentro del mundo profesional de las Artes Escénicas. [*It is now 10 years ago that La Casa Encendida organised the performing arts and disabilities course***. T***he performing arts and disabilities course is part of the professional field of performing arts.*]
2	Original	**Sus solos en directo** son acontecimientos imprevisibles que siempre sorprenden a la audiencia, en ellos interpreta temas de sus álbumes en solitario con partes de improvisación. [**His live solos** *are unpredictable events which always surprise the audience; during these, he performs songs from his albums on his own while improvising some parts.*]
	Simplified	**Los solos en directo de Marc Ribot** siempre sorprenden a la audiencia. En los solos Marc Ribot toca canciones de sus álbumes con partes de improvisación. [**Marc Ribots live solos** *always surprise the audience. During solos, Marc Ribot plays songs from his albums while improvising some parts.*]
3	Original	**Los avisos recibidos por la Gerencia de Emergencias Sanitarias** fueron canalizados a través de las unidades del Servicio Murciano de Salud. [**Calls received by medical emergency services** *were directed by the Department of Health Services in Murcia.*]
	Simplified	**La Gerencia de Emergencias Sanitarias recibieron los avisos**. Las unidades del Servicio Murciano de Salud se encargaron de los avisos. [**The medical emergency services received the calls**. *The Department of Health Services in Murcia took charge of the calls.*]
4	Original	**Ratificación** Experimental [*Experimental* **ratification**]
	Simplified	**Confirmación** Experimental [*Experimental* **confirmation**]
5	Original	Un disolvente **agresivo, muy volátil y que entraña** riesgos para la salud. [*An* **aggressive** *solvent,* **very volatile** *and* **which involves** *health* **risks.**]
	Simplified	El disolvente Percloroetileno puede ser **peligroso** para la salud. [*The solvent perchloroethylene can be* **dangerous** *to your health.*]
6	Original	Lógicamente, al ser menos agresivo, **mejora sustancialmente el tacto de las prendas** y no deja el característico olor a tintorería. [*Logically, due to it being less aggressive,* **it considerably improves how clothes feel** *and does not leave them with that characteristic dry cleaners smell.*]
	Simplified	Otros disolventes, al ser menos agresivos, **dejan la ropa más suave** y no dejan el olor a tintorería. [*Other solvents, due to their being less aggressive,* **make clothes softer** *and don't leave them smelling of dry cleaner.*]

Table 2: Examples of each of our rules (sentence parts altered by applying the corresponding rule are shown in bold)

of this paper and were asked to have sessions no longer than 1 hour so that potential fatigue did not compromise the experiments. In order to minimise potential familiarity effect (texts which already have been simplified are expected to be simplified faster and more efficiently as they are familiar to the writers), we allowed a few days interval between each time a specific text was simplified using different rules. We applied the Spauldings Spanish Readability index – SSR (Spaulding, 1956) as well as the Lexical Complexity index – LC (Anula, 2007) to assess the readability of the simplified texts. Both metrics have shown a good correlation with the possible reading obstacles for various target populations (Štajner and Saggion, 2013), and were used for the evaluation of the automatic TS system in Simplext (Drndarević et al., 2013). We also asked a third writer to simplify samples from the texts used by the first two writers which were pre-assessed to be of comparable complexity, with a view to establishing whether familiarisation has an effect on the output. The results of these readability experiments are presented in Tables 4 and 5 of the following section. We also recorded the time needed to simplify each text as an indication of, among other things, ease of use of (and clarity for) each set of rules and its productivity in general; these results are reported in Tables 6 and 7 of the following section.

Several experiments were conducted to assess the inter-annotator agreement. We believe that the inter-annotator agreement is another good indicator as to how straightforward it is to apply a specific set of simplification rules and how reliable the simplification process is in general. We compute the inter-annotator agreement in terms of the BLEU score (Papineni et al., 2002). BLEU score is widely used in MT to compare the reference translation with the output of the system (translation hypothesis). Here we use the BLEU score to compare the simple sentences produced by one annotator with the corresponding sentences of another annotator. We measure the inter-annotator agreement for all three pairs of annotators (Table 8). In addition, we examined how many times each of the rules was selected by each writer which in our view would be not only a way of accounting for agreement and but also assessing the usefulness of every rule and how balanced a set of rules is in general. Tables 9 and 10 report the results of this study on the texts simplified by all three annotators.

While in the above experiments (which involved only two writers) we made sure that there was at least a few days' span between applying the different sets of rules on the same text, we felt that the risk of familiarity effect could not be removed completely. It is expected that a text which has already been simplified would take less time to be simplified for a second time, even if different rules are applied. Also, as Simplext rules were always applied after our simple rules, we felt that additional experiments were needed where (i) there would be no risk of familiarisation effect and (ii) the rules were applied in a mixed order so that any experience gained from simplification in general cannot serve as unfair advantage to one of the sets of rules. In an experiment seeking to investigate the possible effect of familiarisation in simplification, a third writer simplified a selection of the texts used in the previous experiments by applying each set of rules in a mixed sequence pattern which does not offer any familiarisation nor any advantage of one set of rules over the other. In other words, instead of this writer simplifying the same text twice using different rules, different texts of comparable level of simplicity, informed by the input of the first two writers, were selected and simplified. Based on the results of the time efficiency experiment (Table 6, next section), we chose three pairs (Pair 1, Pair 2 and Pair 3) of texts where for each pair the texts are deemed to be of comparable complexity. By way of example, in Pair 1 which consists of Text 1 and Text 2, Annotator 1 needed the same time for both texts with Simplext rules, and similar time with our simple rules. Annotator 2 needed the same time with our rules, and similar time with Simplext rules. Pair 2 consists of Text 3 and Text 4 and Pair 3 is made of Text 9 and Text 10 for the same reasons as above. The simplification performed by a third writer makes it possible to report readability indices for the text simplified by the third writer, as well as the time taken to simplify, and three-way agreement.

The 10 texts made available by the Spanish news agency Servimedia[10] belong to one of the four following domains: international news (Texts 2, 6, and 10), national news (Texts 4 and 8), society (Texts 3 and 7), or culture (Texts 1, 5, and 9). The sizes of these samples (in sentences and words) are listed in Table 3.

[10]http://www.servimedia.es/

Size	Text 1	Text 2	Text 3	Text 4	Text 5	Text 6	Text 7	Text 8	Text 9	Text 10
Sentences	7	7	5	5	6	4	7	6	5	5
Words	166	183	172	193	176	167	197	180	156	169

Table 3: Size of the texts used for this study

5 Results and discussion

This section presents the results of a study on the readability of texts simplified with our rules as well as with the Simplext rules. It also reports on a time efficiency experiment whose objective is to identify the rules which are less time-consuming to apply. Next, interannotator agreement in terms of BLEU score and selection of rules is discussed and finally, an interpretation of the results of an experiment seeking to establish any familiarisation effect in simplification is provided.

5.1 Readability study

As can be observed from Table 4, simplification performed by our rules improves the readability of texts in almost all cases (note the values in column 'original' with those in columns A-I and A-II for both indices LC and SSR). This improvement was statistically significant in terms of both indices when the texts were simplified by the second annotator, and in terms of the SSR index when the texts were simplified by the first annotator (lower readability indices indicate text which is easier to read).[11].

Text	LC					SSR				
	original	A - I	A - II	B - I	B - II	original	A - I	A - II	B - I	B - II
1	12.00	5.27	6.00	5.57	6.25	183.07	154.67	170.64	147.67	165.70
2	9.76	12.52	9.20	9.74	8.98	174.66	169.07	159.88	161.76	155.99
3	12.95	9.19	8.92	9.04	10.10	176.91	161.30	153.78	157.23	154.80
4	10.74	7.78	7.59	6.53	7.62	179.19	148.27	143.77	133.36	159.26
5	11.79	7.80	9.57	9.47	9.94	196.94	180.05	182.25	164.50	181.99
6	7.23	4.83	4.77	2.00	4.63	177.40	153.22	159.99	130.42	162.19
7	10.23	13.35	8.54	8.29	7.48	175.72	175.11	153.96	137.15	151.34
8	15.14	12.07	11.75	8.96	11.77	191.13	175.42	168.08	155.17	162.59
9	12.86	9.93	10.77	8.87	12.08	178.91	160.47	166.74	142.78	171.08
10	13.52	13.31	10.48	12.03	12.24	166.91	146.96	140.94	152.58	152.94

Table 4: Readability: two readability indices LC and SSR (lower readability indices indicate texts which are easier to read; I and II refer to the two annotators who simplified all 10 texts; A and B refers to the rules which are used: A – ours, B – Simplext)

Text	LC			SSR		
	original	A - III	B - III	original	A - III	B - III
1	12.00	4.92		183.07	170.64	
2	9.76		8.00	174.66		172.58
3	12.95	6.38		176.91	153.78	
4	10.74		7.82	179.19		175.80
9	12.86	10.57		178.91	166.74	
10	13.52		12.15	166.91		154.12

Table 5: Readability of texts simplified by Annotator III (A and B refers to the rules which are used: A – ours, B – Simplext)

[11]Statistical significance was measured by the paired t-test in SPSS at a 0.05 level of significance

The differences in readability between the texts written by employing our simplification rules (columns A-I and A-II) and those written by following the Simplext rules (columns B-I and B-II), were not statistically significant when the simplification was performed by the second annotator, while they were significant when the simplification was performed by the first annotator. When interpreting these results, it is also important to bear in mind that the LC index measures only the lexical complexity of a text, while the SSR index measures general complexity of a text, including both its lexical and its syntactic complexity. We also benefited from the familiarity experiment in which a third annotator was involved, to assess the readability of the simplified versions of the texts of comparable complexity, as produced by the third additional annotator. The results, which are reported in Table 5, suggest that in fact the texts simplified by the third annotator with our rules are easier to read. On the basis of these readability results, it can be concluded that the application of Simplext rules does not necessarily result in a (significantly) simpler version than the one produced by our rules and comparable results are likely to be achieved.

5.2 Time efficiency experiment

The results from the time efficiency experiment (Table 6) show that in all cases, the simplification with our rules is done in shorter (or equal) time. This is also confirmed by the time needed by the third annotator in the additional experiment seeking to establish any familiarity effect (Table 7), where texts of comparable complexity simplified by our rules were simplified faster than the texts simplified with the Simplext rules. In our view, the results of these experiments are indicative not only of the time and cost savings when using our rules but also of our rules being simpler for writers and more straightforward to employ.

Ann.	Set	Text 1	Text 2	Text 3	Text 4	Text 5	Text 6	Text 7	Text 8	Text 9	Text 10
I	A	48	41	30	39	55	29	32	43	24	24
	B	60	60	40	44	44	18	29	19	15	16
II	A	15	15	10	12	30	30	20	15	10	10
	B	30	20	20	15	15	10	10	10	10	10

Table 6: Time efficiency in simplification

Set	Text 1 – Text 2	Text 3 – Text 4	Text 9 – Text 10
A	12	15	11
B	16	16	14

Table 7: Time efficiency in simplification (Annotator III only)

5.3 Inter-annotator agreement and selection of rules

Table 8 presents the inter-annotator agreement in terms of BLEU score. This score accounts for the agreement during the simplification process and the higher the value, the more similar the simplifications performed by the annotators are. In both cases where the difference is significant our rules exhibited a higher degree of agreement among the annotators than the Simplext rules.

Rules	I – II	II – III	I – III
A (Ours)	44.00	52.85	48.27
B (Simplext)	30.46	55.12	33.13

Table 8: Pair-wise inter-annotator agreement in terms of BLEU score

We also analysed how many times each rule was applied by each of the annotators (the annotators were asked to write the numbers of all rules used during simplification of each sentence right after that sentence). We regard the frequency of selection of rules as another indicator for the inter-annotator agreement. Tables 9 and 10 report the frequency of selection of each of our simple rules as well as the Simplext rules for all three annotators (measured only on the texts simplified by all three annotators).

Annotator	Rule 1	Rule 2	Rule 3	Rule 4	Rule 5	Rule 6
I	12	12	5	33	13	9
II	17	14	6	31	10	4
III	15	22	5	16	7	8

Table 9: Frequency of selection of each of our rules (texts 1, 3, and 9)

Rule	Annotator			Rule	Annotator			Rule	Annotator			Rule	Annotator		
	I	II	III		I	II	III		I	II	III		I	II	III
1	25	6	7	**8**	0	1	1	**15**	3	0	0	**22**	0	0	0
2	0	3	1	**9**	0	0	2	**16**	0	0	4	**23**	4	2	1
3	5	0	2	**10**	1	7	2	**17**	0	5	2	**24**	5	0	0
4	19	2	15	**11**	0	0	0	**18**	1	0	0	**25**	0	0	0
5	13	5	0	**12**	0	0	0	**19**	2	1	0	**26**	3	5	0
6	4	0	3	**13**	2	9	0	**20**	1	10	2	**27**	0	0	0
7	1	0	1	**14**	10	6	6	**21**	0	0	0	**28**	1	0	1

Table 10: Frequency of selection of each of the Simplext rules (texts 2, 4, and 10).

It can be seen that there is less difference/discrepancy in the selection of our rules as opposed to the Simplext rules and hence the simplification process can be regarded as more consistent and reliable. Here again, there is higher agreement on our rules as opposed to the Simplext ones. This phenomenon is illustrated in the following example where the annotators used the Simplext rules:

Original: "Esta reforma prevé que todos los delitos relacionados con la seguridad vial (como exceso de velocidad o conducir bajo los efectos del alcohol, las drogas, sin carné o sin puntos) pueden conllevar el decomiso del vehículo, si bien la decisión dependerá del juez."
[This reform will envisage that all crimes related to road safety (such as speeding, driving while under the effects of alcohol or drugs or driving without a licence or points) could result in confiscation of the vehicle, although the decision to do so depends on the judge.]

Annotator 1: "El cambio del Código Penal dice que la decisión de embargar el coche o moto dependerá del juez." (rules used: 5,4,1,4,4)
[The change of the penal code says that the decision to confiscate the car or motorbike depends on the judge.]

Annotator 2: "Esta reforma prevé que todos los delitos relacionados con la seguridad vial como exceso de velocidad o conducir bajo los efectos del alcohol, las drogas, sin carné o sin puntos. Los delitos pueden conllevar la retirada del vehículo pero la decisión dependerá del juez." (rules used: 26,17,20,1,8)
[This reform will envisage that all crimes related to road safety such as speeding or driving under the effects of alcohol, drugs, without a license or points. The crimes could result in confiscation of the vehicle but the decision depends on the judge.]

Annotator 3: "La reforma del Código Penal prevé que todos los delitos relacionados con la seguridad vial pueden dar lugar a la pérdida del vehículo, aunque la decisión dependerá del juez." (rules used: 4,16,4,9)
[The penal code reform will envisage that all crimes related to road safety could result in loss of the vehicle, although the decision depends on the judge.]

5.4 Familiarisation experiment

From the above results, it can be seen that the simplified texts written by the third annotator using a mixed pattern indicate clearer preference to our simple rules in terms of better readability, time efficiency and reliability as opposed to the simplified texts written by Annotator 1 and Annotator 2 where the Simplext texts were applied only at the end. On the basis of this, we conjecture that this difference may be strongly connected with the lingering familiarisation of the annotators when they simplify texts they have already simplified.

6 Conclusions

Simplified texts play an important role in providing accessible and easy-to-understand information for a whole range of users who, due to linguistic, developmental or social barriers, would have difficulty in understanding materials which are not adapted and/or simplified. However, the production of simplified texts can be a time-consuming and labour-intensive task. The results of this study show that a small set of six simple rules, inspired by the concept of Controlled Languages, could produce simplified texts of comparable readability to those produced using a long list of more fine-grained rules such as the ones used in the Simplext project. In addition, the results of this study suggest that our simple rules could be more time-efficient and reliable.

Acknowledgements

We would like to express our gratitude to Horacio Saggion for his help with the resources.

References

A. Anula. 2007. Tipos de textos, complejidad lingüística y facilicitación lectora. In *Actas del Sexto Congreso de Hispanistas de Asia*, pages 45–61.

D. Arnold, L. Balkan, R. Lee Humphreys, S. Meijer, and L. Sadler, 1994. *Machine Translation. An Introductory guide.*, chapter 8, Input, pages 139–155. Blackwell publishers.

S. Cardey. 2009. Controlled Languages for More Reliable Human Communication in Safety Critical Domains. In *Proceedings of the 11th International Symposium on Social Communication, Santiago de Cuba, Cuba, 19-23 January 2009*, pages 330–336.

B. Drndarević, S. Štajner, S. Bott, S. Bautista, and H. Saggion. 2013. Automatic Text Simplication in Spanish: A Comparative Evaluation of Complementing Components. In *Proceedings of the 12th International Conference on Intelligent Text Processing and Computational Linguistics. Lecture Notes in Computer Science. Samos, Greece, 24-30 March, 2013.*, pages 488–500.

G. Freyhoff, G. Hess, L. Kerr, B. Tronbacke, and K. Van Der Veken, 1998. *Make it Simple, European Guidelines for the Production of Easy-toRead Information for People with Learning Disability.* ILSMH European Association, Brussels.

J. Karreman, T. van der Geest, and E. Buursink. 2007. Accessible website content guidelines for users with intellectual disabilities. *Journal of Applied Research in Intellectual Disabilities*, 20:510–518.

R. I. Kittredge, 2003. *Oxford Handbook of Computational Linguistics*, chapter 23, Sub-languages and controlled languages.

Mencap, 2002. *Am I making myself clear? Mencap's guidelines for accessible writing.*

K. Papineni, S. Roukos, T. Ward, and W. Zhu. 2002. BLEU: a method for automatic evaluation of machine translation. In *Proceedings of ACL*, pages 311–318.

PlainLanguage. 2011. Federal plain language guidelines.

H. Saggion, E. Gómez Martínez, E. Etayo, A. Anula, and L. Bourg. 2011. Text Simplification in Simplext: Making Text More Accessible. *Revista de la Sociedad Española para el Procesamiento del Lenguaje Natural*, 47:341–342.

S. Spaulding. 1956. A Spanish Readability Formula. *Modern Language Journal*, 40:433–441.

I. Temnikova. 2012. *Text Complexity and Text Simplification in the Crisis Management domain*. Ph.D. thesis, University of Wolverhampton, UK.

S. Štajner and H. Saggion. 2013. Readability Indices for Automatic Evaluation of Text Simplification Systems: A Feasability Study for Spanish. In *Proceedings of the 6th International Joint Conference on Natural Language Processing (IJCNLP 2013), Nagoya, Japan, 14-18 October 2013*, pages 374–382.

Relative clause extraction for syntactic simplification

Iustin Dornescu, Richard Evans, Constantin Orăsan
Research Group in Computational Linguistics
University of Wolverhampton
United Kingdom
{i.dornescu2,r.j.evans,c.orasan}@wlv.ac.uk

Abstract

This paper investigates *non-destructive simplification*, a type of syntactic text simplification which focuses on extracting embedded clauses from structurally complex sentences and rephrasing them without affecting their original meaning. This process reduces the average sentence length and complexity to make text simpler. Although relevant for human readers with low reading skills or language disabilities, the process has direct applications in NLP. In this paper we analyse the extraction of relative clauses through a tagging approach. A dataset covering three genres was manually annotated and used to develop and compare several approaches for automatically detecting appositions and non-restrictive relative clauses. The best results are obtained by a ML model developed using crfsuite, followed by a rule based method.

1 Introduction

Text simplification (TS) is the process of reducing the complexity of a text while preserving its meaning (Chandrasekar et al., 1996; Siddharthan, 2002a; Siddharthan, 2006). There are two main types of simplification: syntactic and lexical. The focus of syntactic simplification is to take long and structurally complicated sentences and rewrite them as sequences of sentences which are shorter and structurally simpler. Lexical simplification focuses on replacing words which could make reading texts difficult with more common terms and expressions. The focus of this paper is on syntactic simplification and more specifically on how to identify noun post-modifying clauses from complex sentences.

The occurrence of embedded clauses due to subordination and coordination increases the structural complexity of sentences, especially in long sentences where such phenomena are more prevalent. Simple sentences are usually much easier to understand by humans and can be more reliably processed by Natural Language Processing (NLP) tools. Psycholinguistic and neurolinguistic imaging studies show that syntactically complex sentences require more effort to process than syntactically simple ones (Just et al., 1996; Levy et al., 2012). For this reason, complex sentences can cause problems to people with language disabilities. At the same time, previous work indicates that syntactic simplification can improve the reliability of NLP applications such as information extraction (Agarwal and Boggess, 1992; Rindflesch et al., 2000; Evans, 2011), and machine translation (Gerber and Hovy, 1998). In the field of syntactic parsing, studies show that parsing accuracy is lower for longer sentences (Tomita, 1985; McDonald and Nivre, 2011). Therefore, the impact of this paper can be two-fold: on the one hand, it can help increase the accuracy of automatic language processing, and on the other hand, it can be used to make text more accessible to people with reading difficulties.

The research presented in this paper was carried out in the context of FIRST[1], an EU funded project which develops tools to make texts more accessible to people with Autism Spectrum Disorders (ASD). In order to have a proper understanding of the obstacles which pose difficulties to people with ASD, a survey of the literature on reading comprehension and questionnaires completed by people with ASD were

[1]http://first-asd.eu

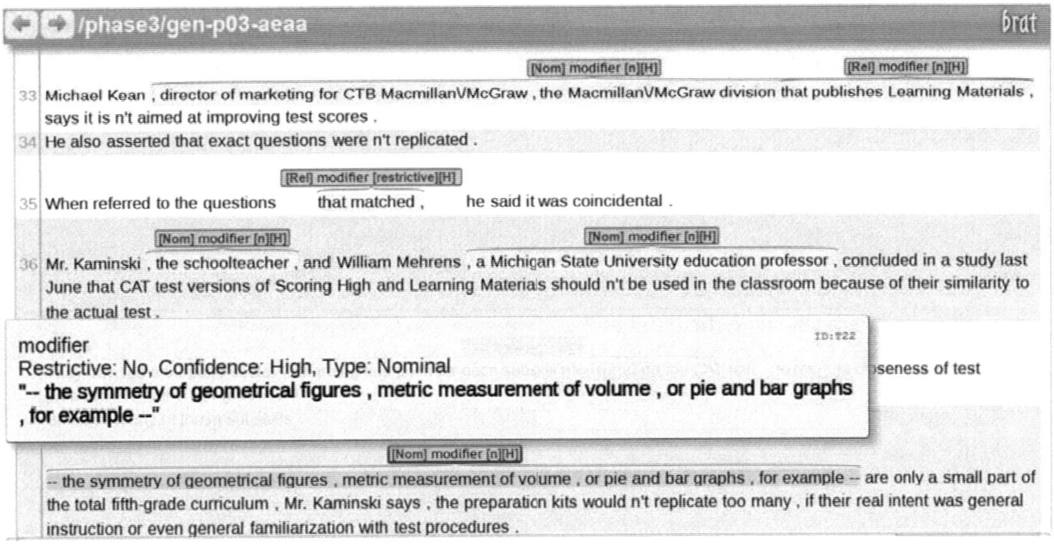

Figure 1: The online annotation using brat

conducted (Martos et al., 2013). The research confirmed that among other types of syntactic complexity, subordinated clauses should be processed by a syntactic simplifier to make the text easier to read.

In this paper, we tackle non-destructive simplification, a form of syntactic simplification in which a clause-based approach is employed to rephrase text in such a way that the meaning of the original text is preserved as much as possible. This is specifically linked to certain types of syntactic structures which can be extracted from the matrix clause without affecting meaning. subordinates, with These types include appositions and non-restrictive relative clauses (Siddharthan, 2002b). This paper presents a method specifically developed for identifying appositions and non-restrictive relative clauses which can be removed from a text without losing essential information.

This paper is structured as follows: Section 2 presents the dataset used to carry out the experiments presented in this paper, including the annotation guidelines and inter-annotator agreement. The machine learning method developed to detect relative clauses is presented in Section 3 and the evaluation results in Section 4. In Section 5, conclusions are drawn.

2 Dataset

To carry out the research presented in this paper, a corpus was annotated. This section presents the annotation guidelines used in the process and discusses issues encountered during the annotation. The annotation was performed using the BRAT[2] tool (Stenetorp et al., 2012). The guidelines were given to the annotators and were explained in a group discussion were several examples were also analysed. Subsequently annotators were given a small set of sentences to trial individually and their questions and feedback led to a revised set of guidelines. Once this training phase was complete, the actual annotation was carried out. The corpus was split randomly each part being annotated by at least two annotators.

2.1 Text genres

The corpus consists of sentences extracted from texts collected in the FIRST project and covers three genres: newswire, healthcare and literature, with some additional sentences from the Penn Treebank (Marcus et al., 1993). The corpus was developed to assist TS for people with ASD (Evans and Orăsan, 2013), following the notion that structurally complex constituents are explicitly indicated by *signs of complexity* such as conjunctions, complementisers and punctuation marks. Evans and Orăsan (2013) developed an annotation scheme and manually labeled these signs.

[2]brat rapid annotation tool `http://brat.nlplab.org/about.html`

Figure 1 shows the interface of the annotation tool. For each annotated span, annotators were asked to fill in three attributes: a) the *type* (relative, nominal, adjectival, verbal, prepositional), b) whether it is *restrictive* (no, yes, unknown) and c) the annotator's *confidence* (low, medium, high). The amount of data in the corpus is listed for each genre in Table 1, i.e. number of sentences and tokens. On average, around half of sentences contain an annotated span, but they occur more frequently in newswire and healthcare than in literature.

Table 1: Corpora used and the total number of annotated spans

Genre (Corpus)	Sentences	Tokens	Spans	Span tokens	Sent. len.	Span len.
healthcare	1214	27379	958	6094	22.55	6.36
news (METER1)	1038	28367	732	5592	27.33	7.64
news (METER2)	1377	37515	1165	9203	27.24	7.90
literature	1946	48620	431	3834	24.98	8.90
News (Penn T.B.)	1733	39740	625	5652	22.93	9.04
Overall	7308	181621	3911	30375	24.85	7.77

2.2 Annotation guidelines

The annotation task involved tagging contiguous sequences of words that comprise post-modifiers of nouns. These are syntactic constituents which follow the head noun in a complex noun phrase (NP), providing additional information about it. We are interested in those post-modifiers which provide additional information but are not part of the parent clause and can be extracted from the sentence without changing its core meaning. These constituents can be either phrases or clauses and are typically bounded by punctuation marks (such as commas, dashes, parentheses) or by functional words (prepositions, relative pronouns, etc.).

The noun post-modifiers of interest are typically clauses or phrases rather than individual words, so not every noun modifier should be marked. Typically they follow the noun phrase whose head they are providing details about and cover several type of subordinated structures (appositions, relative clauses, etc.) In the annotation, the most important aspect is to detect correctly the extent of the annotation (e.g. include surrounding commas). The type is marked as an attribute and evaluated separately. Another attribute indicates whether or not the modifier is a restrictive relative clause.

2.2.1 Restrictive and non-restrictive relative clauses

Restrictive modifiers serve to restrict or limit the set of possible referents of a phrase. In (1a), the subject is restricted to one particular set of chips in a discourse model that may contain many different sets of chips. In (1b), no such restriction is in effect. In this discourse model, all of the chips are made of gallium arsenide and are fragile. Sentences containing restrictive noun post-modifiers require a different method for conversion into a more accessible form than sentences containing non-restrictive noun post-modifiers.

(1) a. *The chips made of gallium arsenide are very fragile* (restrictive)

b. *The chips, which are made of gallium arsenide, are very fragile* (non-restrictive)

Deletion of the noun post-modifier from (1a) produces a sentence that is inconsistent in meaning with the original. All chips, not just the set made of gallium arsenide, are then described as very fragile. When converting sentences with restrictive post-modifiers, it is necessary to generate two sentences: one to put the set of chips made of gallium arsenide into focus and to distinguish this set from the other sets that exist in the discourse model and the other to assert the fact that this set of chips is very fragile. By contrast, deletion of the post-modifier in (1b) produces a sentence that is still consistent in meaning with the original.

In a particular context, it can be quite clear to understand if a specific entity is meant or whether a restricted category of entities is referred to. Normally the sentence is read with two different intonations to indicate the two different meanings (which is why commas usually mark non-restrictive clauses). The presence, or absence of commas should be used to differentiate ambiguous cases in which not enough context is available to decide which is the intended meaning.

(2) a. *They visited two companies today: one in Manchester and one in Liverpool. The company [which is located] in Manchester was remarkable.* (restrictive)

b. *They visited a company and a school. The company, [which is located] in Manchester, was remarkable.* (non-restrictive)

Restrictive relative clauses are also called *integrated, defining* or *identifying* relative clauses. Similarly, non-restrictive relative clauses are called *supplementary, appositive, non-defining* or *non-identifying* relative clauses.

2.2.2 Types of noun post-modifier

Depending on their syntactic function, there are five types of noun post-modifier:

1. **Relative clauses** (usually marked by relative pronouns *who(m), which, that*). These finite clauses are constituents of subclausal elements (noun phrases) within a superordinate clause. They differ from other types of clause such as adverbial clauses, because they are not direct elements of the superordinate clause.[3] They have only an indirect link to the main clause.

(3) *A Bristol hospital that retained the hearts of 300 children who died in complex operations behaved in a "cavalier" fashion towards the parents, an inquiry was told yesterday.*

(4) *The florist [who was] sent the flowers was pleased.*

2. **Nominal-appositives** (which are themselves NPs). Apposition is a relation holding between two NPs (the appositives) in which one serves to define the other. The second NP commonly has a defining role with regard to the first.

(5) *Catherine Hawkins, regional general manager for the National Health Service in the South-west until 1992, appeared before the inquiry yesterday without a solicitor - one should have been provided by the department.*

(6) *My wife, a nurse by training, has helped the accident victim.*

(7) *Goldwater, the junior senator from Arizona, received the Republican nomination in 1964.*

3. **Non-finite clauses** (VP, typically start with an -ing participle or -ed participle verb). These clauses have a non-finite verb and are non-restrictive.[4] These post-modifiers can be regarded as examples of post-modification by a reduced relative clause. To illustrate, in example (8), the non-finite clause is a reduction of the relative clause *who was sitting across from the defendant.*

(8) *Assistant Chief Constable Robin Searle, sitting across from the defendant, said that the police had suspected his involvement since 1997.*

(9) *Lord Melchett led a dawn raid on a farm in Norfolk, causing 17,400 of damage to a genetically modified crop and disrupting a research programme, a court was told yesterday.*

4. **Prepositional phrase post-modification** (PP, typically starting with a preposition). Similar to non-finite clauses, post-modification by PPs, can be regarded as post-modification by 'reduced' relative clauses. For example, the PP in example (10) can be considered a reduction of the relative clause *who is of Chelmsford, Essex.*

[3] In syntax, *elements* are the fundamental units of a clause: subject, verb, object, complement, or adverbial.

[4] They occur in a different tone unit, typically bounded by commas, from the noun head that they modify. They do not restrict or limit the set of possible referents of the complex noun phrase that they modify.

(10) *Boe, of Chelmsford, Essex, admitted six fraud charges and asked for 35 similar offences to be taken into consideration.*

5. **Adjectival post-modification** (AP, including attributes such as height or age). Similar to non-finite clauses, post-modification by adjectival phrases, can be regarded as post-modification by 'reduced' relative clauses. For example, the adjectival phrase in example (11) below can be considered a reduction of the relative clause *who is 58 [years old]*.

(11) *Stanley Cameron, 58 [years old], was convicted in August of 16 counts including vessel homicide and driving under the influence in the November 1997 crash in Fort Lauderdale, Florida.*

(12) *Student Richard, 5ft 10ins tall, has now left home.*

2.3 Annotation insights

The corpus was split into chunks of roughly 100-150 sentences and each was annotated by 2 to 5 annotators. Sentences were randomly selected from the corpus based on length and the presence of signs of complexity (conjunctions, commas, parentheses). Where annotated spans did not match, a reviewer made a final adjudication.

The agreement on detecting the span of post-modifiers was relatively low, on average, the pairwise F1 score was 54.90%. This is mainly because of the way annotators interpreted the instructions. For example, some annotators systematically marked all parenthetical expressions whereas others never did this. The most frequent error was omission of relevant post-modifiers; annotators typically reached higher precision than recall. This suggests a systematic disagreement which affects files annotated by few annotators. A way to address this problem is by aggregating all annotated spans for each document and asking annotators to confirm which of them are indeed post-modifiers. This is being carried out in a separate study, where a voting scheme is used to mitigate the recall problem.

Looking only at the cases where two annotators marked the same span as a post-modifier, we can investigate the level of agreement reached on the individual attributes: *type* and *restrictiveness*. Annotators reached high pairwise agreement (kappa=0.78) when marking the type of the post-modifier. This suggests that the beginning of the post-modifiers has reliable markers which could be used to automatically predict type. The pairwise agreement for restrictiveness is lower (kappa=0.51), but still good, considering that the two values are not equally distributed (70% of post-modifiers are non restrictive). Possible causes of this are: lack of context (sentences were extracted from their source documents), lack of domain knowledge (where the post-modifers are not about entities, but specialised terminology, such as symptoms, procedures, strategies).

Although agreement on the two attributes can be improved, the biggest challenge is to ensure that all post-modifiers are annotated, i.e. to address situations when only one annotator marks a span. One common cause of disagreement concerns noun modifiers within the same NP, such as prepositional phrases. For example:

(13) *The $2.5 billion Byron 1 plant near Rockford was completed in 1985.*

While this span modifies a noun, it is part of the NP itself, and it is arguably too short to be relevant for rephrasing the sentence in a TS system; it is more likely a candidate for deletion as is the case with sentence compression systems.

Another frequent issue concerns nested modifiers, where annotators usually marked only one of the possible constituents. A related issue is how to deal with nested and overlapping spans, not only from the point of view of the guidelines, but also in the way the annotation is used in practice.

(14) *The new plant, located in Chinchon, **about 60 miles from Seoul,** will help meet increased demand.*

An interesting debate concerns ambiguous constituents which can have several interpretations. In the previous sentence, the second constituent *about 60 miles from Seoul* can be considered an apposition modifying the proper noun *Chinchon*, or a prepositional phrase modifying the verb *located*; both entail a similar meaning to a human reader. This example illustrates a situation which frequently occurs in natural language text: for stylistic or editorial reasons writers omit words which are implied by the context. The effect is that the syntactic structure becomes ambiguous, but the information communicated to the reader is nevertheless unaffected. This issue also suggests that distinguishing the type of a post-modifier (i.e. relative, nominal, adjectival, verbal, prepositional) only reflects its form and less so its role. For example, it is easy to rephrase most post-modifiers as relative clauses, e.g.:

(15) a. Nominal-appositives: *My wife,* ***who is*** *a nurse by training, has helped the accident victim.*

b. Verbal-appositives: *Lord Melchett led a dawn raid on a farm in Norfolk,* ***which caused*** ~~*causing*~~ *17,400 of damage... , a court was told yesterday.*

c. Prepositional-appositives: *Boe,* ***who lives in*** ~~*of*~~ *Chelmsford, Essex, admitted six fraud charges and asked for 35 similar offences to be taken into consideration.*

d. Adjectival-appositives: *Student Richard,* ***who is*** *5ft 10ins tall, has now left home.*

During the annotation process there were several issues raised by the annotators, both seeking clarifications of the guidelines as well as identifying new situations in the corpus. A conclusion of the feedback we gathered is that the most important decision is whether a post-modifier is restrictive or not, as this will lead to different strategies for rephrasing the content in order to preserve the meaning as much as possible. The type can be deduced based on the first tokens in the post-modifier.

3 Detection of relative clauses

In this paper we follow the sign complexity scheme introduced by Evans and Orăsan (2013), where punctuation marks and functional words are considered explicit markers of coordinated and subordinated constituents, the two syntactic mechanisms leading to structurally complex sentences.

The signs of syntactic complexity comprise conjunctions (*[and], [but], [or]*), a complementiser (*[that]*), wh-words (*[what], [when], [where], [which], [while], [who]*), *punctuation marks ([,], [;], [:])*, and 30 compound signs consisting of one of these lexical items immediately preceded by a punctuation mark (e.g. *[, and]*). These signs are automatically tagged with a label indicating type of constituent they delimit, such as finite clauses (EV) or strict appositives (MN), and the position of the sign, such as start/left boundary (SS*) or end/right boundary (ES*). For example, the label ESMA indicates end of an adjectival phrase. An automatic tagger for signs of syntactic complexity was developed using a sequence tagging approach (Dornescu et al., 2013) and is used in this work to select complex sentences from the corpus and to provide linguistic information to the proposed approach.

The two baselines used are rule based systems for detecting post modifiers. System RC1 uses a set of rules to detect appositives which are delimited by punctuation marks and do not contain any verbs. Such expressions are typically nominal appositives or parenthetical expressions e.g.

(16) a. The chief financial officer, Gregory Barnum, announced the merger in an interview.

b. Oxygen can be given with a face mask or through little tubes (nasal cannulae or 'nasal specs') that sit just under your nostrils.

c. The business depends heavily on the creativity of its chief designer, Seymour Cray.

3.1 Rule-based approach

The second baseline used as a reference, DAPR (Detection of Adnominal Post-modifiers by Rules), is a component of a text simplification system for people with autistic spectrum disorders (Evans et al., 2014). Although the system can also rephrase complex sentences, in this paper we only used the appositive constituents detected in a sentence by DAPR.

It employs several hand-crafted linguistic rules which detect the extent of appositions based on the presence of signs of syntactic complexity, in this case punctuation marks, relative pronouns, etc. DAPR exploits rules and patterns to convert sentences containing noun post-modifiers such as finite clauses (EV), strict appositives (MN), adjective phrases (MA), prepositional phrases (MP), and non-restrictive non-finite clauses (MV) into a more accessible form.

The conversion procedure is implemented as an iterative process. When a pattern matches the input sentence, the detected post-modifier is deleted and the resulting sentence is then processed. The priority of each pattern determines the order in which they are matched when processing sentences which contain multiple left boundaries of relevant constituents (i.e. signs of complexity tagged with certain labels). The patterns are implemented to match the first (leftmost) sign of syntactic complexity in the sentence.

The rules used to convert sentences containing noun post-modifiers exploit patterns to identify both the noun post-modifier and the preceding part of the matrix NP, which can be used to re-phrase the post-modifier as a coherent, stand-alone sentence. Table 3 provides examples of patterns and the strings that they match for each class of signs serving as the left boundary of a noun post-modifier. The patterns are expressed using terms described in Table 2.

Table 2: Terms used in the patterns

Element	Description
w_v	Verbal words, including –ed verbs tagged as adjectives
w_n	Nominal words
w_a	Adjectival words with POS tags JJ, JJS, and VBN
w_{nmod}	Nominal modifiers: adjectives, nouns
w_{nspec}	Nomimal specifiers: determiners, numbers, possessive pronouns
w_{POS}	Word with part-of-speech tag POS (from the Penn Treebank tagset (Santorini, 1990) utilised by the part of speech tagger distributed with the LT TTT2 package)
CLASS	Sign of syntactic complexity of functional class CLASS (Evans and Orăsan, 2013).
"	Quotation marks
B-F	Sequences of zero or more characters

Table 3: Rules used to used to detect noun post-modifiers

Type	Rule	Trigger pattern & Example
SSEV	61	$w_{IN}\ w_{DT}^{*}\ w_n\ \{wn \vert of\}^{*}$ SSEV w_{VBD} C sb "* *But he was chased for a mile-and-a-half by a passer-by who gave police a description of the Citroen driver.*
	7	$w_{\{n \vert DT\}}^{*}\ w_n$ SSEV B ESCCV *Some staff at the factory, which employed 800 people, said they noticed cuts on his fingers.*
SSMA	81	$w_{NNP}^{*}\ w_{NNP}$ SSMA $w_{\{RB \vert CD\}}^{*}\ w_{CD}$ ESMA w_{VBD} *Matthew's pregnant mum Collette Jackson, 24, collapsed sobbing after the pair were sentenced.*
	83	$w_{NNP}^{*}\ w_{NNP}$ SSMA w_{CD} ESMA *The court heard that Khattab, 25, a trainee pharmacist, confused double strength chloroform water with concentrated chloroform.*
SSMN	6	$w_{\{NNP \vert NNPS\}}^{*}\ w_{\{n \vert a\}}^{*}\ w_n$ SSMN B ESMN *Mr Justice Forbes told the pharmacists that both Mr Young and his girlfriend, Collette Jackson, 24, of Runcorn, Cheshire, had been devastated by the premature loss of their son.*
	3	$w_{\{DT \vert PRP\$\}}\ \{w_{\{n \vert a\}} \vert of\}^{*}\ w_n$ SSMN B ESMN *Police became aware that a car, a VW Golf, was arriving in Nottingham from London.*
SSMP	4	$w_{\{NNP \vert NNPS\}}^{*}\ w_{\{NNP \vert NNPS\}}$ SSMP "* w_{IN} B ESMP *Justin Rushbrooke, for the Times, said: "We say libel it is, but it's a very, very long way from being a grave libel.*
	1	$w_{\{NNP \vert NNPS\}}^{*}\ w_{\{NNP \vert NNPS\}}\ \{is \vert are \vert was \vert were\}\ w_{CD}$ SSMP w_{IN} B ESMA *In the same case Stephen Warner, 33, of Nottingham, was jailed for five years for possession of heroin with intent to supply.*
SSMV	12	$w_{PRP}\ w_{RB}^{*}\ w_{VBD}$ B SSMV $w_{RB}^{*}\ w_{VBG}$ C $\{sb \vert \}$ *He attended anti-drugs meetings with Nottinghamshire police, sitting across from Assistant Chief Constable Robin Searle.*
	2	$w_{\{NNP \vert NNPS\}}^{*}\ w_{\{NNP \vert NNPS\}}$ SSMV $w_{\{VBG \vert VBN\}}$ B ESMV *Andrew Easteal, prosecuting, said police had suspected Francis might be involved in drugs and had begun to investigate him early last year.*

The underlined examples in Table 3 mark only the noun post-modifier. The patterns also identify the preceding part of the matrix NP (in square brackets in the example below). The rules include substitutions of indefinite articles by demonstratives or definite articles. Following the method applied to sentences containing noun post-modifiers, rule SSEV-63 would convert:

(17) *But he was chased for a mile-and-a-half by a passer-by who gave police a description of the driver.*

Into the more accessible sequence of sentences:

(18) a. *But he was chased for a mile-and-a-half by [a passer-by].*

b. *[That passer-by] gave police a description of the driver.*

3.2 ML-based approach

As many types of appositive modifiers are simple in structure, we also follow a tagging approach for the task of detecting noun post-modifiers. We employ the common IOB2 format where the beginning of each noun post-modifier is tagged as `B-PM` and tokens inside it are tagged as `I-PM`. All other tokens are tagged as other: `O`. This is similar to a named entity recognition or to a chunking task where only one type of entity/chunk is detected. For comparison we compare the performance of the approach with a rule based method for detecting appositive post-modifiers.

The corpus was used to build two supervised tagging models based on Conditional Random Fields (Lafferty et al., 2001): CRF++[5] and crfsuite[6]. Four feature sets were used. Model A contains standard features used in chunking, such as word form, lemma and part of speech (POS) tag. Model B adds the predictions of baseline system RC1 as an additional feature: using the IOB2 models, tokens have one of three values: B-RC1, I-RC1 or O-RC1. Similarly, model C adds the predictions of baseline system DAPR also using the IOB2 approach. This allows us to test whether the baseline systems are robust enough to be employed as input to the sequence tagging models. Model D adds information about the tokens of the sentence which are signs of syntactic complexity. These are produced automatically.

4 Results and analysis

Results reported by `conlleval`[7], the standard tool for evaluating tagging, are presented in Table 4. Although the two baselines, RC1 and DAPR, out-perform the CRF++ models, the best overall performance is achieved by the crfsuite models.

The rules employed by the RC1 baseline can be misled by sentences containing enumerations, numerical expressions and direct speech due to false positive matches. Although few and addressing the simplest post-modifiers, the rules perform well.

The more complex baseline, DAPR, appears to be more conservative (it makes the fewest predictions overall), which suggests it covers fewer types of appositions than covered by our dataset. Compared to the previous baseline, DAPR detects more complex appositions and relative clauses with better precision, but with reduced recall.

Although the CRF models also use as features the predictions made by the two baseline models, due to the level of noise, the improvement is small, between 1 and 2 points. Adding information about the tagged signs of syntactic complexity actually has a negative impact on both models, suggesting that the signs are less relevant for this type of syntactic constituent. A large difference in performance is noted between the two CRF tools: whereas CRF++ is outperformed by both baselines, crfsuite achieves much better performance despite using the same input features.

To gain better insights into the performance of the best model, Table 5 presents label-wise results. Given that the average length of a post-modifier is 7, inside tokens (I-PM) are 7 times more prevalent than beginning tokens (B-PM). Despite this, the model achieves similar performance for both (F1 score just below 0.60). The two tables also bring evidence suggesting that detecting the end token of a post-modifier is challenging: although the start is correctly detected for 48.89% of appositives, only 39.94%

[5]`http://crfpp.googlecode.com/svn/trunk/doc/index.html`

[6]`http://www.chokkan.org/software/crfsuite/`

[7]`http://www.cnts.ua.ac.be/conll2000/chunking/conlleval.txt`

Table 4: Results reported by `conlleval` on the test set (90076 tokens, 2098 annotated post-modifiers)

		#predicted phrases	**#correct phrases**	**accuracy**	**precision**	**recall**	**F1**
RC1	baseline	1287	371	81.01	28.83	17.68	21.92
DAPR	baseline	535	163	81.25	30.47	7.77	12.38
CRF++	A:word & POS	3372	289	85.48	8.57	13.78	10.57
	+B:RC1 predictions	3381	315	85.66	9.32	15.01	11.50
	+C:DAPR predictions	3586	319	85.63	8.90	15.20	11.22
	+D:tagged signs	3680	319	85.60	8.67	15.20	11.04
crfsuite	A:word & POS	1391	790	87.54	56.79	37.65	45.29
	+B:RC1 predictions	1437	825	87.55	**57.41**	39.32	46.68
	+C:DAPR predictions	1470	**838**	87.56	57.01	**39.94**	**46.97**
	+D:tagged signs	1481	**838**	87.56	56.58	**39.94**	46.83

are a perfect match. This suggests that more work is necessary to improve the ability to detect post-modifiers but also to better determine their correct extent. The second part is critical to the perceived performance of the TS system, as incorrect detection usually leads to incorrect text being generated for users, whereas a loss in recall may be transparent.

Table 5: Label-wise performance for the best model (crfsuite C)

label	**#match**	**#model**	**#ref**	**precision**	**recall**	**F1**
O	70452	77884	73955	90.46	95.26	92.80
B-PM	1014	1469	2074	69.03	48.89	57.24
I-PM	7406	10723	14047	69.07	52.72	59.80
		Macro-average		76.18	65.63	69.95

5 Conclusions

The paper presents a new resource for syntactic text simplification, a corpus annotated with relative clauses and appositions which can be used to develop and evaluate non-destructive simplification systems. These systems extract certain types of syntactic constituents and embedded clauses and rephrase them as stand-alone sentences to generate less structurally complex text while preserving the meaning intact. A supervised tagging model for automatic detection of appositions was built using the corpus and will be included in a text simplification system.

Acknowledgements

The research described in this paper was partially funded by the European Commission under the Seventh (FP7-2007-2013) Framework Programme for Research and Technological Development (FP7-ICT-2011.5.5 FIRST 287607). We gratefully acknowledge the contributions of all the members of the FIRST consortium for their feedback and comments, and to the annotators for their useful insights.

References

Rajeev Agarwal and Lois Boggess. 1992. A simple but useful approach to conjunct identification. In *Proceedings of the 30th Annual Meeting on Association for Computational Linguistics*, ACL '92, pages 15–21, Stroudsburg, PA, USA. Association for Computational Linguistics.

R. Chandrasekar, Christine Doran, and B. Srinivas. 1996. Motivation and Methods for Text Simplification. In *Proceedings of the 16th conference on Computational linguistics - Volume 2*, pages 1041–1044.

Iustin Dornescu, Richard Evans, and Constantin Orăsan. 2013. A Tagging Approach to Identify Complex Constituents for Text Simplification. In Galia Angelova, Kalina Bontcheva, and Ruslan Mitkov, editors, *Proceedings of Recent Advances in Natural Language Processing, RANLP'13*, pages 221 – 229, Hissar, Bulgaria. RANLP 2011 Organising Committee / ACL.

Richard Evans and Constantin Orăsan. 2013. Annotating signs of syntactic complexity to support sentence simplification. In Ivan Habernal and Vclav Matoušek, editors, *Text, Speech, and Dialogue*, volume 8082 of *Lecture Notes in Computer Science*, pages 92–104. Springer Berlin Heidelberg.

Richard Evans, Constantin Orăsan, and Iustin Dornescu. 2014. An evaluation of syntactic simplification rules for people with autism. In *Proceedings of the 3rd Workshop on Predicting and Improving Text Readability for Target Reader Populations (PITR)*, pages 131–140, Gothenburg, Sweden, April. Association for Computational Linguistics.

Richard J. Evans. 2011. Comparing methods for the syntactic simplification of sentences in information extraction. *LLC*, 26(4):371–388.

Laurie Gerber and Eduard H. Hovy. 1998. Improving translation quality by manipulating sentence length. In David Farwell, Laurie Gerber, and Eduard H. Hovy, editors, *AMTA*, volume 1529 of *Lecture Notes in Computer Science*, pages 448–460. Springer.

M. A. Just, P. A. Carpenter, and K. R. Thulborn. 1996. Brain activation modulated by sentence comprehension. *Science*, 274:114–116.

John Lafferty, Andrew McCallum, and Fernando Pereira. 2001. Conditional random fields: Probabilistic models for segmenting and labeling sequence data. In *Proceedings of the 18th International Conference on Machine Learning*, pages 282–289.

J. Levy, E. Hoover, G. Waters, S. Kiran, D. Caplan, A. Berardino, and C. Sandberg. 2012. Effects of syntactic complexity, semantic reversibility, and explicitness on discourse comprehension in persons with aphasia and in healthy controls. *American Journal of Speech–Language Pathology*, 21(2):154 – 165.

Mitchell P. Marcus, Beatrice Santorini, and Mary Ann Marcinkiewicz. 1993. Building a large annotated corpus of english: The penn treebank. *Computational Linguistics*, 19(2):313–330.

Juan Martos, Sandra Freire, Ana Gonzlez, David Gil, Richard Evans, Vesna Jordanova, Arlinda Cerga, Antoneta Shishkova, and Constantin Orasan. 2013. User preferences: Updated report. Technical report, The FIRST Consortium.

Ryan McDonald and Joakim Nivre. 2011. Analyzing and integrating dependency parsers. *Comput. Linguist.*, 37(1):197–230, March.

Thomas C. Rindflesch, Jayant V. Rajan, and Lawrence Hunter. 2000. Extracting molecular binding relationships from biomedical text. In *ANLP*, pages 188–195.

Beatrice Santorini. 1990. Part-Of-Speech tagging guidelines for the Penn Treebank project (3rd revision, 2nd printing). Technical report, Department of Linguistics, University of Pennsylvania, Philadelphia, PA, USA.

A. Siddharthan. 2002a. An architecture for a text simplification system. *Language Engineering Conference, 2002. Proceedings.*

Advaith Siddharthan. 2002b. Resolving Attachment and Clause Boundary Ambiguities for Simplifying Relative Clause Constructs. *Association for Computational Linguistics Student Research Workshop*, pages 60–65.

Advaith Siddharthan. 2006. Syntactic simplification and text cohesion. *Research on Language and Computation*, 4:77–109.

Pontus Stenetorp, Sampo Pyysalo, Goran Topić, Tomoko Ohta, Sophia Ananiadou, and Jun'ichi Tsujii. 2012. Brat: A web-based tool for nlp-assisted text annotation. In *Proceedings of the Demonstrations at the 13th Conference of the European Chapter of the Association for Computational Linguistics*, EACL '12, pages 102–107, Stroudsburg, PA, USA. Association for Computational Linguistics.

Masaru Tomita. 1985. *Efficient Parsing for Natural Language: A Fast Algorithm for Practical Systems*. Kluwer Academic Publishers, Norwell, MA, USA.

Exploring the effects of Sentence Simplification on Hindi to English Machine Translation System

Kshitij Mishra **Ankush Soni** **Rahul Sharma** **Dipti Misra Sharma**
Language Technologies Research Centre
IIIT Hyderabad
{kshitij.mishra,ankush.soni,rahul.sharma}@research.iiit.ac.in,
dipti@iiit.ac.in

Abstract

Even though, a lot of research has already been done on Machine Translation, translating complex sentences has been a stumbling block in the process. To improve the performance of machine translation on complex sentences, simplifying the sentences becomes imperative. In this paper, we present a rule based approach to address this problem by simplifying complex sentences in Hindi into multiple simple sentences. The sentence is split using clause boundaries and dependency parsing which identifies different arguments of verbs, thus changing the grammatical structure in a way that the semantic information of the original sentence stay preserved.

1 Introduction

Cognitive and psychological studies on 'human reading' state that the effort in reading and understanding a text increases with the sentence complexity. Sentence complexity can be primarily classified into 'lexical complexity' and 'syntactic complexity'. Lexical complexity deals with the vocabulary practiced in the sentence while syntactic complexity is governed by the linguistic competence of native speakers of a particular language. In this respect, the modern machine translation systems are similar to humans. Processing complex sentences with high accuracy has always been a challenge in machine translation. This calls for automatic techniques aiming at simplification of complex sentences both lexically and syntactically. In context of natural language applications, lexical complexity can be handled significantly by utilizing various resources like lexicons, dictionary, thesaurus etc. and substituting infrequent words with their frequent counterparts. However, syntactic complexity requires mature endeavors and techniques.

Machine Translation systems when dealing with highly diverges language pairs face difficulty in translation. It seems intuitive to break down the sentence into simplified sentences and use them for the task. Phrase based translation systems exercise a similar approach where system divides the sentences into phrases and translates each phrase independently, later reordering and concatenating them into a single sentence. However, the focus of translation is not on producing a single sentence but to preserve the semantics of the source sentence, with a decent readability at the target side.

We present a rule based approach which is basically an improvement on the work done by (Soni et al., 2013) for sentence simplification in Hindi. The approach adapted by them has some limitations since it uses verb frames to extract the core arguments of verb; there is no way to identify information like time, place, manner etc. of the event expressed by the verb which could be crucial for sentence simplification. A parse tree of a sentence could potentially address this problem. We use a dependency parser of Hindi for this purpose. (Soni et al., 2013) didn't consider breaking the sentences at finite verbs while we split the sentences on finite verbs also.

This paper is structured as follows: In Section 2, we discuss the related work that has been done earlier on sentence simplification. Section 3 addresses criteria for classification of complex sentences. In section 4, we discuss the algorithm used for splitting the sentences. Section 5 outlines evaluation of the systems using both BLEU scores and human readability . In Section 6, we conclude and talk about future work in this area.

2 Related Work

Siddharthan (2002) presents a three stage pipelined approach for text simplification. He has also looked into the discourse level problems arising from syntactic text simplification and proposed solutions to overcome them. In his later works (Siddharthan, 2006), he discussed syntactic simplification of sentences. He has formulated the interactions between discourse and syntax during the process of sentence simplification. Chandrasekar et al. (1996) proposed Finite state grammar and Dependency based approach for sentence simplification. They first build a stuctural representation of the sentence and then apply a sequence of rules for extracting the elements that could be simplified. Chandrasekar and Srinivas (1997) have put forward an approach to automatically induce rules for sentence simplification. In their approach all the dependency information of a words is localized to a single structure which provides a local domain of influence to the induced rules.

Sudoh et al. (2010) proposed divide and translate technique to address the issue of long distance reordering for machine translation. They have used clauses as segments for splitting. In their approach, clauses are translated separately with non-terminals using SMT method and then sentences are reconstructed based on the non-terminals. Doi and Sumita (2003) used splitting techniques for simplifying sentences and then utilizing the output for machine translation. Leffa (1998) has shown that simplifying a sentence into clauses can help machine translation. They have built a rule based clause identifier to enhance the performance of MT system.

Though the field of sentence simplification has been explored for enhancing machine translation for English as source language, we don't find significant work for Hindi. Poornima et al. (2011) has reported a rule based technique to simplify complex sentences based on connectives like subordinating conjunction, relative pronouns etc. The MT system used by them performs better for simplified sentences as compared to original complex sentences.

3 Complex Sentence

In this section we try to identify the definition of sentence complexity in the context of machine translation. In general, complex sentences have more than one clause (Kachru, 2006) and these clauses are combined using connectives. In the context of machine translation, the performance of system generally decreases with increase in the length of the sentence (Chandrasekar et al., 1996). Soni et al. (2013) has also mentioned that the number of verb chunks increases with the length of sentence. They have also mentioned the criteria for defining complexity of a sentence and the same criteria is apt for our purpose also. We consider a sentence to be complex based on the following criteria:

- Criterion1 : Length of the sentence is greater than 5.
- Criterion2 : Number of verb chunks in the sentence is more than 1.
- Criterion3 : Number of conjuncts in the sentence is greater than 0.

Table 1 shows classification of a sentence based on the possible combinations of 3 criteria mentioned above.

4 Sentence Simplification Algorithm

We propose a rule based system for sentence simplification, which first identifies the clause boundaries in the input sentence, and then splits the sentence using those clause boundaries. Once different clauses are identified, they are further processed to find shared argument for non-finite verbs. Then, the Tense-Aspect-Modality(TAM) information of the non-finite verbs is changed. Below example (12) illustrates the same,

Table 1: Classification of a sentence as simple or complex

Criterion1	Criterion2	Criterion3	Category
No	No	No	Simple
No	No	Yes	Simple
No	Yes	No	Simple
No	Yes	Yes	Simple
Yes	No	No	Simple
Yes	No	Yes	Complex
Yes	Yes	No	Complex
Yes	Yes	Yes	Complex

(1) raam ne khaanaa khaakara pani piya
Ram food after+eating water drink+past
'Ram drank water after eating.'

We first mark the boundaries of clauses for example (12). 'raam' and 'khaanaa' are starts, and 'khaakara' and 'piya' are ends of two different clauses respectively. Once the start and end of clauses are identified we break the sentence into those clauses. So for above example, the two clauses are:

1. 'raam ne pani piya'

2. 'khaanaa khaakara'

Once we have the clauses, we post process those clauses which contain non-finite verbs, and add the shared argument and TAM information for these non-finite clauses. After post-processing, the two simplified clauses are:

1. 'raam ne pani piya.'

2. 'raam ne khaanaa khaayaa.'

4.1 Algorithm

Our system comprises of a pipeline incorporating various modules. The first module determines the boundaries of clauses (clause identification) and splits the sentence on the basis of those boundaries. Then, the clauses are processed by a gerund handler - which finds the arguments of gerunds, shared argument adder which fetches the shared arguments between verbs, TAM(Tense Aspect Modality) generator which changes the TAM of other verbs on the basis of main verb. The figure 4.1 shows the data flow of our system, components of which have been discussed in further detail in this section.

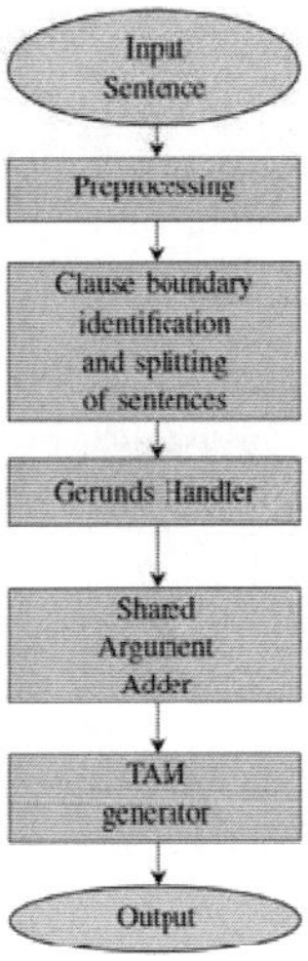

Figure 1: Data Flow

4.1.1 Preprocessing

In this module, raw input sentences are processed and each lexical item is assigned a POS tag, chunk and dependency relations information in SSF format(Bharati et al., 2007; Bharati et al., 2009). We have used (Jain et al., 2012) dependency parser for preprocessing. Example (2) shows the output of this step.
Input sentence:

(2) raam ne khaanaa khaayaa aur paani piyaa.
Ram+erg food eat+past and water drink+past
'Raam ate food and drank water'

Output: Figure (1) shows the different linguistic information in SSF format. Tag contains the Chunk and POS information of the sentence, and drel in feature structure stores different dependency relations in a sentence.

Offset	Token	Tag	Feature structure
1	((	NP	<fs name='NP' drel='k1:VGF'>
1.1	raama	NNP	<fs af='raama,n,m,sg,3,d,0,0'>
1.2	ne	PSP	<fs af='ne,psp,,,,,'>
	))		
1 2	((	NP	<fs name='NP2' drel='k2:VGF'>
2.1	khaanaa	NN	<fs af='khaanaa,n,m,sg,3,d,0,0' name='khaanaa'>
	))		
3	((	VGF	<fs name='VGF' drel='ccof:CCP'>
3.1	khaayaa	VM	<fs af='KA,v,m,sg,any,,yA,yA' name='khaayaa'>
	))		
4	((	CCP	<fs name='CCP'>
4.1	aur	CC	<fs af='Ora,avy,,,,,' name='aur'>
	))		
5	((	NP	<fs name='NP3' drel='k2:VGF2'>
5.1	paani	NN	<fs af='pAnI,n,m,sg,3,d,0,0' name='paani'>
	))		
6	((	VGF	<fs name='VGF2' drel='ccof:CCP'>
6.1	piyaa	VM	<fs af='pIyA,unk,,,,,' name='piyaa'>
	))		

Figure 1: SSF representation for example 2

4.1.2 Clause boundary Identification and splitting of sentences

This module takes the input from preprocessing module and identifies the clause boundaries in the sentence. Once clause boundaries are identified, the sentence is divided into different clauses. We have used the technique mentioned in Sharma et al. (2013) which has shown how implicit clause information present in dependency trees/relations can be used to extract clauses from a sentence. Once we mark the clause boundaries using this approach, we break the sentence into different simple clauses along those clause boundaries. The example(3) given below illustrates the same.

(3) raam jisne khaanaa khaayaa ghar gayaa
Ram who+rel. food eat+past home go+past
'Ram who ate food, went home'

Example(3) with clause boundaries marked is, (raam (jisne khaanaa khaayaa) ghar gayaa). Once the clause boundaries are marked, we break the sentence using those boundaries. So for Example(3), split clauses are,

1. raam ghar gayaa.
2. jisne khaanaa khaayaa.

4.1.3 Gerunds Handler

Since, Sharma et al. (2013) identifies clause boundary for non-finite and finite verb only, gerunds are not handled in the previous module. This module is used to handle gerunds in the given sentence. In this module, the gerund chunks are first indentified and then further processed after getting the arguments. Consider an example:

(4) logon ko sambodhit karne ke baad dono netaon ne pradhanmantri ko istifa saunpa
people address doing after both leaders Prime minister to resignation gave
'After addressing people, both leaders gave resignation to the prime minister'

In the above example, the clause boundary identifier module marks the entire sentence as a clause but *karne ke baad* is a gerund chunk (verb chunk) here, which is marked as VGNN according to the tagset of the POS tagger used. According to definition of complex sentence given in section 3 gerunds also introduce complexity in a sentence. Therefore, in order to simplify such sentences, we use dependency parsing information for extracting the arguments of gerund and splitting the sentence.

Here *logon ko* and *sambodhit* are the arguments of verb chunk *karne ke baad*. Here *ke baad* is postposition of verb *karne* so, *ke baad* is splitted from *karne* and it has been used with the pronoun *is* to make the sentence more readable.

1. *logon ko sambodhit karne*
2. *iske baad dono netaon ne pradhanmantri ko istifa saunpa*

4.1.4 Shared Argument Adder

After identifying clauses and handling gerunds, the shared arguments are identified between the verbs and sentences are formed accordingly. For example:

(5) (ram (chai aur paani peekar) soyaa)
(ram (tea and water after drinking) slept)
'ram slept after drinking tea and water'

Here *ram* is the shared argument(k1-karta) of both the verbs *peekar* and *soyaa* . The dependency parser used, marks the inverse dependencies for shared arguments which helps in . So the output of this module is:

1. *ram chai aur paani peekar.*

2. *ram soyaa.*

4.1.5 TAM generator

The split sentences given by the above module are converted into more readable sentences using this module. The form of other verbs is changed using TAM information of the main verb provided by the morph, as shown in Figure 1. For example:
INPUT:

1. *ram chai aur paani peekar.*

2. *ram soyaa.*

OUTPUT:

1. *ram chai aur paani peeyaa.*

2. *ram soyaa.*

Here *soyaa* is the main verb having *yaa* as TAM. Word generator[1] has been used to generate the final verb given root form of the verb and TAM of the verb. Here *pee* is the root form of *peekar* and *yaa* is given as the TAM. Word generator generates *peeyaa* as the final word which is used in the sentence.

5 Evaluation

We have taken a corpus of 100 complex sentences for the evaluation of our tool. These sentences were taken from the Hindi treebank (Bhatt et al., 2009; Palmer et al., 2009). Evaluation of both sentence simplification and its effects on google MT system for Hindi to English(google translate) was performed. The evaluation of sentence simplification is a subjective task which considers both readability and preservation of semantic information. Hence both manual as well as automatic evaluations have been performed.

5.1 Automatic Evaluation

We have used BLEU score (Papineni et al., 2002) for automatic evaluation of both tasks; sentence simplification and enhancing MT system. Higher the BLEU score, closer the target set is to the reference set. The maximum attainable value is 1 while minimum possible value is 0. For our Automatic evaluation we adopted the same technique as Specia (2010) using BLEU metric. We have achieved 0.6949 BLEU score for sentence simplification task. For MT system, we have evaluated the system with and without sentence simplification tool. It was observed that the system with sentence simplification tool achieved 0.4986 BLEU score whereas the system without sentence simplification gave BLEU score of 0.4541.

5.2 Human Evaluation

To ensure the simplification quality, manual evaluation was also done. 20 sentences were randomly selected from the testing data-set of 100 sentences. Output of these 20 sentences, from the target set were manually evaluated by 2 subjects, who have done basic courses in linguistics, for judging 'Readability' and 'Simplification' quality on the scale of $0 - 3$, 0 being the worst and 3 being the best.
For Simplification performance, scores were given according to following criteria :

[1]Taken from the ILMT pipeline.

- 0 = None of the expected simplifications performed.
- 1 = Some of the expected simplifications performed.
- 2 = Most of the expected simplifications performed.
- 3 = Complete Simplification.

After taking input from all the participants the results averaged out to be 2.5.
For Human evaluation of MT system, the subjects had to select the better translation between system with sentence simplification tool and system without it. The subjects reportedly observed a better translation of the system with sentence simplification tool. It was reported that 12 out of 20 sentences were translated better after being simplified, and quality of 3 remained unchanged.

Translation quality of 5 was reported to be better before simplification. This happened because the system breaks the sentences at every verb chunk it encounters, which in some cases makes the sentence lose its semantic information.

For example the sentence below contains five verb chunks. The system breaks the sentence into five sentences.:

(6) *yah poochne par ki kya we dobaara congress mein lautenge sangama ne kaha ki na*
this ask on that what he again Congress in return Sangama told that neither
to iski zarurat hai aur na hi peeche lautane ka sawal hi uthta hai
then its requirement is and nor back return question raises is
'On asking whether he would return again in Congress, Sangma replied that neither there is need of this nor there is the question of reverting back.'

System's Output

1. (7) kya we dobaara congress mein lautenge
what he again Congress in return
'Would they return again in Congress ?'

2. (8) yah poochane par sangama ne kaha
this ask on Sangama told
'On asking this, Sangama said.'

3. (9) na to iski zarurat hai
neither its requirement is told
'Neither it is needed.'

4. (10) na hee peeche lautana hai
neither back return is
'Neither he will return.'

5. (11) iska sawal uthta hai
its question raises is
'The question arises.'

It is clearly observable that the simplified sentences failed to preserve the meaning of the original sentence. Further, the system does not change the *vibhakti* (Bharati et al., 1995) of the simplified sentences which, in some cases makes the sentence lose its meaning. For example

(12) machharon ke katne ke baad wo beemar hue
Mosquitoes of bite of after they sick became
'They became sick after being bitten by the mosquitoes.'

System's Output:

1. (13) machharon ke kata
   Mosquitoes of bite
   'Not a valid sentence'

2. (14) is ke baad wo beemar hue
   this of after they sick became
   'After this they became sick.'

In the first simplified sentence the *vibhakti "ke"* should have been changed to *"ne"* for the formation of a valid sentence.

6 Conclusion and Future Work

As shown in the results, after simplifying the sentences, BLEU score of the translation increases by 4.45. The manual evaluation also got encouraging results in simplification and readability with a score of **2.5** on a scale of $0 - 3$. There is a clear indication that our tool can enhance the performance of MT for complex sentences by simplifying them. Future work will include minimizing the lose of semantic information while splitting the sentences and making simplified sentences more readable and grammatically correct. In addition to extending the system, evaluating the impact of our tool on other NLP tasks like parsing, dialog systems, summarisation, question-answering systems etc. is also a future goal.

Acknowledgements

We would like to thank Riyaz Ahmad Bhat, Rishabh Shrivastava and Prateek Saxena for their useful comments and feedback which helped us to improve this paper and Anshul Bhargava, Arpita Batra, Abhijat Sharma, Gaurav Kakkar, Jyoti Jha and Urmi Ghosh for helping us in annotation.

References

Akshar Bharati, Vineet Chaitanya, Rajeev Sangal, and KV Ramakrishnamacharyulu. 1995. *Natural language processing: a Paninian perspective*. Prentice-Hall of India New Delhi.

Akshar Bharati, Rajeev Sangal, and Dipti M Sharma. 2007. Ssf: Shakti standard format guide. pages 1–25.

Akshara Bharati, Dipti Misra Sharma, Samar Husain, Lakshmi Bai, Rafiya Begam, and Rajeev Sangal. 2009. Anncorra: Treebanks for indian languages, guidelines for annotating hindi treebank.

R. Bhatt, B. Narasimhan, M. Palmer, O. Rambow, D.M. Sharma, and F. Xia. 2009. A multi-representational and multi-layered treebank for hindi/urdu. In *Proceedings of the Third Linguistic Annotation Workshop*, pages 186–189. Association for Computational Linguistics.

Raman Chandrasekar and Bangalore Srinivas. 1997. Automatic induction of rules for text simplification. *Knowledge-Based Systems*, 10(3):183–190.

Raman Chandrasekar, Christine Doran, and Bangalore Srinivas. 1996. Motivations and methods for text simplification. In *Proceedings of the 16th conference on Computational linguistics-Volume 2*, pages 1041–1044. Association for Computational Linguistics.

Takao Doi and Eiichiro Sumita. 2003. Input sentence splitting and translating. In *Proc. of Workshop on Building and Using Parallel Texts, HLT-NAACL 2003*, pages 104–110.

Naman Jain, Karan Singla, Aniruddha Tammewar, and Sambhav Jain, 2012. *Proceedings of the Workshop on Machine Translation and Parsing in Indian Languages*, chapter Two-stage Approach for Hindi Dependency Parsing Using MaltParser, pages 163–170. The COLING 2012 Organizing Committee.

Yamuna Kachru. 2006. *Hindi*, volume 12. John Benjamins Publishing.

Vilson J Leffa. 1998. Clause processing in complex sentences. In *Proceedings of the First International Conference on Language Resources and Evaluation*, volume 1, pages 937–943.

M. Palmer, R. Bhatt, B. Narasimhan, O. Rambow, D.M. Sharma, and F. Xia. 2009. Hindi Syntax: Annotating Dependency, Lexical Predicate-Argument Structure, and Phrase Structure. In *The 7th International Conference on Natural Language Processing*, pages 14–17.

Kishore Papineni, Salim Roukos, Todd Ward, and Wei-Jing Zhu. 2002. Bleu: a method for automatic evaluation of machine translation. In *Proceedings of the 40th annual meeting on association for computational linguistics*, pages 311–318. Association for Computational Linguistics.

C Poornima, V Dhanalakshmi, Anand M Kumar, and KP Soman. 2011. Rule based sentence simplification for english to tamil machine translation system. *International Journal of Computer Applications*, 25(8):38–42.

Rahul Sharma, Soma Paul, Riyaz Ahmad Bhat, and Sambhav Jain. 2013. Automatic clause boundary annotation in the hindi treebank.

Advaith Siddharthan. 2002. An architecture for a text simplification system. In *Language Engineering Conference, 2002. Proceedings*, pages 64–71. IEEE.

Advaith Siddharthan. 2006. Syntactic simplification and text cohesion. *Research on Language and Computation*, 4(1):77–109.

Ankush Soni, Sambhav Jain, and Dipti Misra Sharma. 2013. Exploring verb frames for sentence simplification in hindi. Proceedings of the Sixth International Joint Conference on Natural Language Processing, pages 1082–1086. Asian Federation of Natural Language Processing.

Lucia Specia. 2010. Translating from complex to simplified sentences. In *Computational Processing of the Portuguese Language*, pages 30–39. Springer.

Katsuhito Sudoh, Kevin Duh, Hajime Tsukada, Tsutomu Hirao, and Masaaki Nagata. 2010. Divide and translate: improving long distance reordering in statistical machine translation. In *Proceedings of the Joint Fifth Workshop on Statistical Machine Translation and MetricsMATR*, pages 418–427. Association for Computational Linguistics.

Automatic Text Simplification For Handling Intellectual Property (The Case of Multiple Patent Claims)

Svetlana Sheremetyeva
National Research South Ural State University, pr. Lenina 76, 454080 Chelyabinsk, Russia
LanA Consulting ApS, Moellekrog 4, Vejby, 3210, Copenhagen, Denmark
lanaconsult@mail.dk

Abstract

Handling intellectual property involves the cognitive process of understanding the innovation described in the body of patent claims. In this paper we present an on-going project on a multi-level text simplification to assist experts in this complex task. Two levels of simplification procedure are described. The macro-level simplification results in the visualization of the hierarchy of multiple claims. The micro-level simplification includes visualization of the claim terminology, decomposition of the claim complex structure into a set of simple sentences and building a graph explicitly showing the interrelations of the invention elements. The methodology is implemented in an experimental text simplifying computer system. The motivation underlying this research is to develop tools that could increase the overall productivity of human users and machines in processing patent applications.

1 Introduction

In today's highly-competitive marketplace much of industrial companies' true worth relates to intellectual property protected by patents. However, a great deal of patents is not used to raise standards across industries as much as they could. In US alone more than 95% of all active patents are not licensed to a single third party and do not earn the first dollar of licensing revenue. Part of the problem is that patents can be difficult to understand and value as they are written in dense, arcane legal language that only a technical expert can read (http://patentproperties.com/patentinnovations.html).

Moreover, even patent experts, whose task is to conduct analysis of patent documents, e.g., for novelty, scope of protection or value can spend quite a time and effort to clearly understand a crucial part of a patent document, claims. The patent claim is the only part of a patent that defines the scope of inventor's rights. Linguistically the claim is the most difficult information carrier. Patent law demands the claim to be written as a single albeit very complex and long sentence, no matter that it might run for a page or so. Figure 1 shows a short fragment of a claim, just to illustrate what is said above.

Claim 1. A grinding tool for profile strips of wood or the like, comprising a plurality of grinding segments arranged in at least two rows; at least two base bodies, each associated with one of said rows of said grinding elements, said base bodies being movable relative to one another, said grinding segments of one of said rows being offset relative to said grinding segments of the other of said rows so that said rows of said grinding segments are insertable into one another over at least a part of a respective length thereof;.....and clamping means including two clamping elements associated with and located at each side of a respective one of said base bodies so as to engage said grinding segments, said two clamping elements including an inner clamping element which is basket-shaped and has a plurality of webs which are spaced from one another by respective angular distances and lie under said grinding segment receivers, and another clamping element which has a plurality of intermediate spaces into which said webs of said inner basket-shaped clamping element are insertable.

Figure 1. A fragment of Claim1 of the US patent 4,777,771. This patent has 24 claims.

The limited space of this paper does not allow us enclosing in the current description a real life patent claim section, but an interested reader can consult any patent bank site.

This problem of patent expertise is further complicated by the fact that a patent document, as a rule, contains not just one but a large number of claims that should be read and interpreted as a whole. Anybody who has seen patent claims at least once will find it unnecessary to calculate claim readability indices to get persuaded that the claim text is extremely low readable. Traditional readability formulas normally take into account the number of words per sentence or/and the number of "hard", be it long or low frequency, words per sentence (Kincaid, Fishburne, Rogers, & Chissom, 1975; Brown, 1998; Greenfield, 2004). Both the first and the second ratio will be equal to the number of words in a claim sentence where practically all words are "hard" terms, some of them used for the first time. The same goes for the claim syntactic structure.

Patent experts attending to their examination tasks normally perform simplification of a claim text manually. Evidently, there is a great need for tools that could automate this process. The need has already attracted attention of R&D groups working in the field of text processing. Given the linguistic complexity of the claim it is not surprising that practically all reports related to the patent/claim simplification research describe on-going projects rather than completed studies or development (see Section 2 for references). In this paper we attempt to complement existing achievements by presenting our research in the area and suggest text simplification techniques to facilitate understanding/readability of both, the whole section of multiple claims in a patent document, and an individual claim.

The specificity of our approach is primarily motivated and conditioned by the fact that in patent examination patent experts cannot afford analyzing a simplified claim text where the content has been changed during the simplification procedure. Not a single word in the claim could be changed or omitted. Even the use of synonyms, let alone the omission of claim structural elements (pruning), can change the scope of the invention and result in patent infringement and, hence, court cases. All these put our work out of the mainstream in the text simplification research. However it meets the definition of text simplification as a process of making the text more comprehensible for a targeted audience. It should be also noted that though this study is primarily addressed to patent experts, our simplification solutions might be useful for both laypeople and machines meant to automatically process patents, e.g., information retrieval or machine translation systems.

The rest of the paper is organized as follows. Section 2 is devoted to related work. Section 3 discusses challenges in the field of claim simplification. Section 4 describes our approach to claim simplification on a macro-level that addresses the whole body of multiple patent claims. In sections 4 and 5 we suggest some solutions to the simplification of a single claim, which we call a micro-level simplification. Further in Section 6 we present evaluation results and summarize our on-going research in Conclusions.

2 Related work

Research on automatic text simplification aims at developing techniques and tools that could make texts more comprehensible for certain types of targeted audience/readers. The mainstream of text simplification is developing methodologies and tools for general types of texts that address people with special needs, such as poor literacy readers (Aluisio et al. 2010), readers with mild cognitive impairment (Dell'Orletta et al., 2011), elderly people (Bott et al., 2012), language learners of different levels (Crossley and McNamara, 2008) or just "regular" readers (Graesser et al., 2004). Text simplification is most often performed on the sentence level. Simplifying texts to provide more comprehensible input to a targeted audience the developers generally work within two approaches: an intuitive approach and a structural approach. An intuitive approach relies mainly on the developers' intuition and experience (Allen, 2009) that leads to using less lexical diversity, less sophisticated words, less syntactic complexity, and greater cohesion. A structural approach depends on the use of structure and word lists that are predefined by the intelligence level, as typically found in targeted readers. The latter is defined by readability formulas. Traditional readability formulas are simple algorithms that measure text readability based on sentence length and word length. Later research on readability suggests formulas that reflect the psycholinguistic and cognitive processes of reading (Crossley et al.2011).

At the linguistic level, simplified texts are largely modified to control the complexity of the lexicon and the syntax. Automated text simplification tools are trying to achieve this purpose by combining linguistic and statistical techniques and penalize writers for polysyllabic words and long, complex sentences. (Siddharthan, 2002) describe the implementation of the three stages - analysis, transformation and regeneration, system that lay particular emphasis on the discourse level aspects of syntactic simplification. Some works on text simplification use parallel corpora of original and simplified sentences (Petersen & Ostendorf, 2007). There are works where text simplification is treated as a "translation task within a RBMT (Takao and Sumita. 2003). In (Specia, 2010) text simplification is developed in the Statistical Machine Translation framework, given a parallel corpus of original and simplified texts, aligned at the sentence level. In (Poornima et al.2011) a rule based technique is proposed to simplify the complex sentences based on connectives like relative pronouns, coordinating and subordinating conjunctions. Sentence simplification is expressed as the list of sub-sentences that are portions of the original sentence. (Bott, et al., 2012) describe a hybrid automatic text simplification system which combines a rule based core module with a statistical support module that controls the application of rules in the wrong contexts.

The approaches to patent claim simplification can be roughly put into two groups. Studies of the first group try to adapt to the patent domain general text simplification techniques and involve lexical and/or structural substitution, pruning, paraphrasing, etc. For example, in (Shinmori et al., 2003) the discourse structure of the patent claim is built by means of a rule-based technique; each discourse segment is then paraphrased. In (Mille and Wanner, 2008) the claim sentence (by means of lexical and punctuation clues) is segmented into clausal units, that are then compressed into a summary. The simplification methods proposed by this group of researches to some extent change the original content of the claim that might not always be desirable, especially for patent experts.

Another group of studies focuses on segmenting, reformatting or highlighting certain parts of the patent claim without changing the content of the original. For example, in one of the earlier works a rule-based technique was developed for decomposing the complex sentence of a claim into a set of simple sentences while preserving the initial content (Sheremetyeva, 2003). Most recently (Shinmori et al., 2012) suggested aligning claim phrases with explanatory text from the description section, while (Ferraro et al., 2014) proposed an approach that involves highlighting the claim segments borders and reformatting the original text so as to emphasis segments with the identified border marker. This approach does not involve any syntactic restructuring, just visualization of claim segments.

In general, due to the linguistic complexity of patent claims all research on automatic claim simplification make extensive use of rule-based methods possibly augmented with statistical techniques. Text segmentation is performed on two levels. First the claim in segmented into 3 information-relevant parts, the preamble, transition and body and then the claim body is further segmented into smaller parts, often clausal structures.

To the best of our knowledge practically all publications on claim simplification consider individual claims, while in real life most patents contain multiple interrelated claims of different types and a patent reader has to understand the whole range of information in the claim section. The cited studies address laypeople that are not trained to read patent claims. However, there is also a great demand for claim readability tools among patent experts who have to perform thorough and tedious work on claim analysis for different examination tasks on a daily basis. When accessing the prototype systems or methodologies, the developers normally evaluate the correctness of their own intuitive understanding how a simplified claim should look. No studies on end-user requirements or user-centered evaluation have been reported so far. In our work among others we have tried to address the above issues.

Our research includes the following steps:

- Extraction of expert knowledge about their needs and procedure of claim analysis
- Acquisition of linguistic knowledge about the patent claim sublanguage
- Developing a prototype claim simplification system that meets expert expectations.

3 Challenges in claim simplification

In preparing for this research we have investigated professional instructions (Pressman. 2006; Radack, 1995) on how to read patent claims and conducted extensive interviews with patent experts of several companies in the US and Europe handling intellectual property[1]. The recommendations are as follows. The first step towards understanding a claim is to identify its information parts, preamble, transition and the body. Another recommendation is to identify and mark the elements of the invention spelled

[1] The confidentiality policy of these companies does not allow us discosing them in this paper.

out in the body of the claim. Element markup is useful not only for proper understanding of the claim but also because claims have to be supported by the description. Any terms used in claims must be found in the description. Hence, there is a demand to automate patent terminology extraction that could underlie terminology markup, e.g., by highlighting.

In real practice the examiners manually decompose the claim in a tree with noun terminology and predicates (verbs, adjectives and prepositions) on separate indented lines to clearly see the invention elements and their interrelations. Hence there is a need to automate the construction of such element-relation diagrams for every particular claim. The experts we have interviewed were also very enthusiastic about a tool that could decompose a complex claim sentence into a set of simple sentences-features of the invention, provided the content of the claim is preserved. It is evident that building such a tool is a much more demanding task than any other as it clearly cannot rely on statistical methods only but also requires extensive linguistic knowledge and rule-based techniques.

Most of patents contain a large number of claims that can claim experts have to interpret related to each other. There are two basic types of claims: the *independent claims*, which stand on their own, and the *dependent claims*, which depend on one or several claims and should be interpreted in conjunction with their parents. Any dependent claim which refers to more than one other claim is a *multiply dependent claim* that should also be visualized in a simplifying tool.

Based on the extracted expert demands and analyzing procedures we suggest two levels of patent claim simplification that should necessarily preserve the claim section content:

- the macro-level simplification resulting in the visualization of the hierarchy of claims explicitly showing their interdependence (type: dependent/independent, parents and children)
- the micro-level simplification of one claim that includes
  - visualization of the claim terminology
  - decomposition of a claim complex structure into a set of simple sentences
  - building a diagram explicitly showing the interrelations of invention elements.

The micro-level claim simplification is extremely challenging as cannot but require the NLP techniques and elaborate and extensive linguistic resources that for our purpose do not exist so far.

4 Macro-level simplification

The macro-level simplification improves the readability of the whole section of multiple claims in a patent document. For this purpose we have developed a patent macro-analyzer that takes as input a whole patent document and outputs the hierarchy of claims with a lot of accompanying information relevant for patent examination. In particular, the macro-analyzer automatically performs the following successive steps:

- Segmentation of the claim section from the rest of the input patent document
- Segmentation of individual claims from the body of the claim section
- Identification of the type of every segmented claim as independent or dependent
- Identification of all children (one or multiple) for every individual claim
- Identification of all parents (one or multiple) for every dependent claim
- Construction of an hierarchical tree of claims

The macro-analyzer is rule-based and uses the knowledge extracted from a 9mio wordform corpus of US and European patents[2] in the English language. The knowledge for macro-simplification is very shallow and it includes:

Clues signaling on the start of the Claims section such as location (the claim section of a patent comes after the description at the end of the patent document) and a list of delimiting expressions, such as *"We claim», » I claim», » claim", "what we claim is"*, etc.

Clues signaling on the start of every individual claim that include numbering, formatting, punctuation and a list of delimiting expressions. The claims are set forth as separately numbered paragraphs in

[2] This is justified by the similarity of structures of different national patents due to the similarity of writing rules imposed by Patent Law throughout the world.

a single-sentence format. Each claim begins with a capital letter and with a number. The first claim of an issued patent is always numbered "1," with each claim thereafter following in an ascending sequence of Arabic numerals (1, 2, and 3) from broad claims to narrow claims.

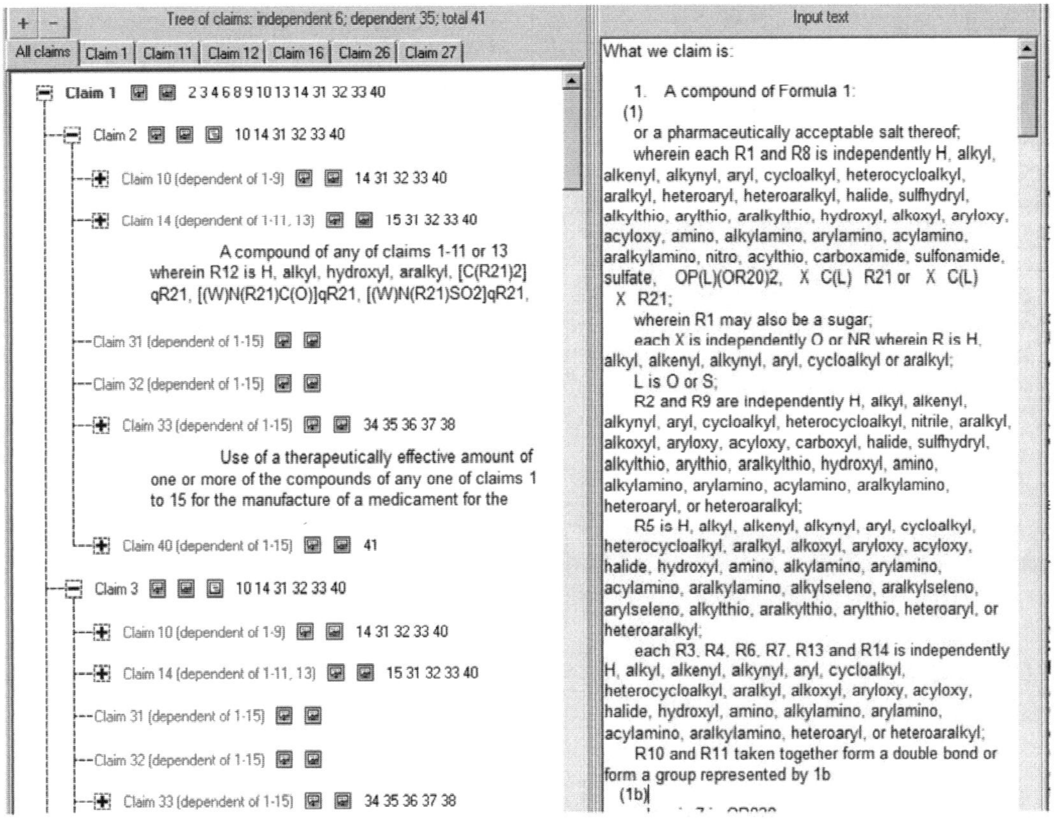

Figure.2. A screenshot of the tree of claims fragment visualized in the user interface. The number of dependent and independent claims is shown on the top. The right pane is an interactive window which displays the input patent text; this text can be scrolled and/or edited right in there. The left pane shows a tree with claims as nodes. Clicks on the coloured square buttons next to claim nodes allow displaying/hiding the claim text The numbers on the right of a claim node list claims dependent on the claim in question. The tree of claims is collapsible and expendable in different ways. The "+" and "-"are the usual "expand" and "collapse" tree buttons. The coloured square buttons on the right allow getting truncated sub-trees of the main claim tree.

Clues signaling on the dependent claim that include a list of reference expressions. The text of a dependent claim always starts with a number (this clue is common to all types of claims) and a specific reference expression of the type "2. The machine of Claim 1,..." . The wording of a multiply dependent claim reference expression could be, for example, "5. A gadget according to claims 3 or 4, further comprising...". Multiply dependent claims may depend on other claims which do not necessarily follow one another. For example, dependent claims can be referenced as "14. A compound of any of claims 1-9 or 13,...." There may be also reference expressions like "17. An invention as in previous claims...". Though variable, the number of dependent claim reference expressions is still limited, so that they can be rather exhaustively acquired and explicitly listed in the analyzer knowledge base.

Clues signaling on the parents of dependent claims that are in fact contained in the *dependent claims* reference expressions. The sets of parents of different dependent claims can be different, the same or intersect. That does not always let build a single root tree of claims for a patent. In complicated cases the macro-analysis can result in a forest of root trees of claims.

Clues signaling on the children of the claims that do not need to be acquired, the analyzer calculates them from the dependent claims reference expressions.

The type of knowledge required for macro-analysis of the claim section and high structural similarity of national patents imposed by Patent law make the analysis algorithm practically language-independent. The only thing which is required to port the macro-analyzer from English into any other language is to change the lexicon of reference expressions. Such lexicons should certainly be acquired for every particular language by corpus analysis, which is pretty straight forward.

The macro-analyzer is implemented as a module of an end-user tool that visualizes the results of macro-analysis in the form of a tree structure as shown in Figure 2. The visualized tree is highlighted in a way that facilitates the understanding of multiple claim interrelations and allows grasping a lot of claim-related information "at a glance" thus improving the readability of the claim section. The independent claims in the tree nodes are highlighted in blue, while dependent claims are presented in red. Lists of children are displayed in black to the right of their parent claim nodes, the parents of a multiply dependent claims are shown in red on the left of multiply-dependent claim nodes. The nodes corresponding to multiply-dependent claims are highlighted in red. The interface program does supplementary math and displays a total number of claims, as well as the number of independent and dependent claims, correspondingly, and displays them in the status bar. The independent claims are bookmarked.

The user can navigate the claim tree, which can collapse/expand in different combinations to display the subtrees of independent claims, claim children, parents, or ascenders. There are special buttons next to each claim node that allow to partially or fully display claim texts. The input text of a whole patent is displayed on the right interactive pane of the interface. These functionalities allow interactively aligning claims with certain parts of the description for consistency check or editing. The macro-analyzer for the English language is currently available as a standalone tool.

5 Micro-level claim simplification

5.1 The knowledge

Micro-level simplification at each of its stages is done by means of a specific combination of rule-based and statistical techniques and relies on linguistic knowledge of different depth. This knowledge is structured following the methodology described in (Sheremetyeva, 1999; Sheremetyeva, 2003) and is mostly coded in the system lexicon as well as in analysis and generation rules. Different modules of the micro-level simplification component use specific parts and types of linguistic knowledge included in the lexicon and their own specific sets of rules.

The word list for the lexicon was automatically acquired from a 9 million-word corpus of a US and European patents available to us from our previous projects and patent web sites. A semi-automatic supertagging procedure was used to label these lexemes with their supertags. A supertag codes morphological information (such as POS and inflection type) and semantic information, an ontological concept, defining a word membership in a certain semantic class (such as object, process, substance, etc.). For example, the supertag Nf shows that a word is a noun in singular (N), means a process (f), and does not end in –ing. This supertag will be assigned, for example, to such words as `activation` or `alignment`. At present we use 23 supertags that are combinations of 1 to 4 features out of a set of 19 semantic, morphological and syntactic features for 14 parts of speech. For example, the feature structure of noun supertags is as follows: Tag [POS[Noun [object [plural, singular] process [-ing, other[plural, singular]] substance [plural, singular] other [plural, singular]]]]].

The "depth" of supertags is specific for every part of speech and codes only that amount of the knowledge that is believed to be sufficient for our analysis procedure. The units of the system lexicon are described with a different level of depth. A deep (information-rich) description is only assigned to predicates. Other types of lexemes are only assigned morphological information.

Predicates in our system are words, which are used to describe interrelations between the elements of the invention. They are mainly verbs, but can also be adjectives or prepositions. A predicate entry covers both the lexical, and, crucially for our system, the syntactic and semantic knowledge. The morphological knowledge includes partial paradigms of explicitly listed predicate wordforms as found in the patent corpora. Syntactic and semantic knowledge relevant for our task is included in the CASE_ROLEs and PATTERNs fields of predicate entries. The CASE_ROLEs field lists a set of the corpus-based predicate case-roles such as agent, theme, place, instrument, etc. The PATTERNs code domain-based information on the most frequent co-occurrences of predicates with their case-roles, as well as their linear order in the claim text. For example, the pattern (1 x 3 x 2) corresponds to such clam fragment as `1:boards x:are 3:rotatably x:mounted 2:on the pillars.`

The processing algorithms and rules for every stage of micro-simplification will be described in the corresponding sections below.

5.2 Terminology visualization

The readability of patent claims increases if the reader can spot the terminology at a glance. It is important not only in the process of claim examination for novelty but also for a quick check of whether the claim text complies the writing rules prescribed by the Patent law. Claims have to be supported by the patent description, which means that any terms used in the claims must be found in the description. To facilitate these tasks we simplify the claim text by automatically highlighting its nominal terms with the subsequent highlighting of these terms in the patent description. In case a certain claim term is not found in the description a warning message is given. This task is performed based on the results of a shallow analysis performed by a hybrid NP extractor and NP and predicate term chunkers which in succession run on the same claim text.

To extract (and then highlight) nominal terminology we use the NP extractor described in (Sheremetyeva, 2009). The extraction methodology combines statistical techniques, heuristics and a very shallow linguistic knowledge extracted from the main system lexicon (see Section 5.1). The NP extractor knowledge base consists of a number of unilingual lexicons, - sort of extended lists of stop words forbidden in particular (first, middle or last) positions in a typed lexical unit (NP in our case). These lists of stopwords are automatically extracted from the morphological zones of the entries of relevant parts-of-speech.

The NP extraction procedure starts with n-gram calculation and then removes those n-grams that cannot be NPs from the list of all calculated n-grams. This is done by successive matching the components of calculated n-grams against the stop lexicons. The NP extraction itself thus neither requires such demanding NLP procedures, as tagging, morphological normalization, POS pattern match, etc., nor does it rely on statistical counts (statistical counts are only used to sort out keywords which is not needed in our case). The advantages of this extractor are in that it does not rely on a preconstructed corpus, works well on small texts, does not miss low frequency units and can reliably extract *all* NPs from an input text. The noun phrases thus extracted are of 1 to 4 components due to the limitations of the extractor that uses a 4-gram model. A small adaptation of the extractor has been made to have it better suite the current task. First, we excluded a lemmatizer from the original extraction algorithm and kept all extracted NPs in their textual forms and, second, we updated the tool knowledge so as to allow NPs being extracted form a claim text with articles and determiners (“said”, this”, etc;) if present. It was done to avoid the ambiguity in the subsequent NP chunking in the claim text.

The chunker users the knowledge dynamically produced by the extractor (lists of all NPs with determiners in their text form as found in the claim text in question). The NPs are chunked in the claim text by matching the extractor output against the claim text. The predicate terminology is chunked by the main lexicon predicate entries look-up practically without (ambiguity) problems. The chucked nominal and predicate terminology is visualized in the user interface by highlighting them in the claim text (see Figure 3, left pane). The same dynamic knowledge is used to check for the claim noun and predicate terminology in the text of the description. In case of a failure a warning message about inconsistency is displayed.

5.3 One-sentence-to-many decomposition

Decomposition of one syntactically complex claim sentence into a set of simple sentences is done in two takes. First the claim is segmented into the preamble, transition and body text, and then the preamble and claim body are further segmented into simple sentences.

The first segmentation is pretty straight forward and is performed based on the knowledge about transition expressions explicitly listed in the system knowledge base. The list of corpus-based transition expressions covers both the US and European rules for writing claims. In the US claims the transitions basically used are: "comprising", "which comprises," "consisting of," and "consisting essentially of." Modern claims follow a format whereby the preamble is separated from the transitional term by a comma, while the transitional term is separated from the body by a colon.

Under the European Patent Convention a claim can be written according to the so-called "two-part form" where the claim text is divided into a generic part that contains old knowledge and a difference part that contains novel features of the invention. The delimiting expressions are "characterized in that" or "characterized by". If the European format is used, what is called the "preamble" is different from the meaning of «preamble" under the U.S. patent law. In an independent claim in Europe, the preamble is everything which precedes the delimiting expression. The preamble in Europe is sometimes also called "pre-characterizing portion". It can contain a text of a certain length and syntactic complexity. The preamble can therefore require decomposition (simplification) as well.

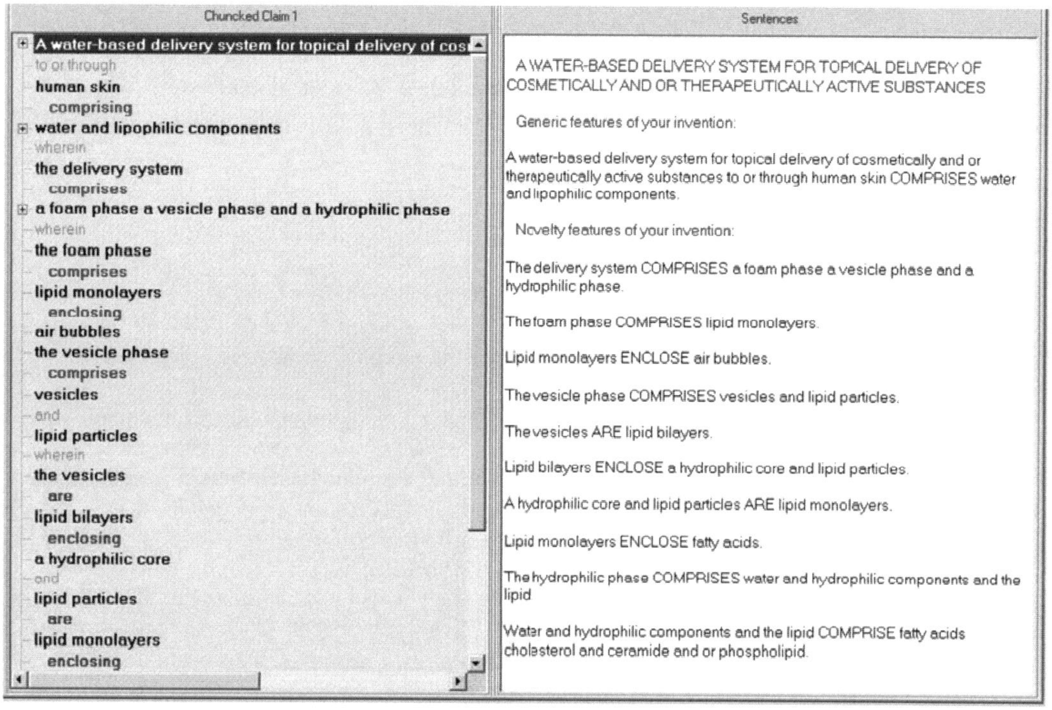

Figure 3. A screenshot of "Decomposition" page of the user interface. The left pane shows the input claim text with highlighted terminology. Predicates are in blue, the nominal terminology is boldfaced. The right pane visualizes a simplified claim text in the form of simple sentences. The content of the texts in both panes is the same.

Decomposition of the generic/preamble and difference/body parts of the claim text demands much more sophisticated techniques than those used at previous levels of simplification. It is performed by the deep analyzer that in full uses the knowledge of the lexicon described in Section 5.1.

The deep analyzer includes a disambiguating supertagger, typed phrase chunker based on PSG rules and DPG-based predicate/argument dependency identifier. It superficially performs the NLP analysis procedure as described in (Sheremetyeva 2003). However, the original procedure of the NLP claim analysis presented in the cited paper was significantly modified and simplified by introducing the shallow analyzer (see section 5.2) at the pre-deep-NLP analysis stage. This made the analysis procedure more robust and less computationally demanding.

The workflow of the current analyzing procedure is as follows. A raw claim is first pre-processed by the shallow analyzer that extracts and chunks claim nominal phrases and predicates as presented in Section 5.2.

The claim, thus partially parsed and tagged is then input into the preexisting deep analyzer, which completes super tagging, recursive chunking and defines predicate/argument dependencies. The output of the analyzer is a shallow interlingual representation where the content of every nascent simple sentence is represented by a separate predicate/argument structure (proposition) in the form

proposition::={label predicate-class predicate ((case-role)(case-role))}*
case-role::= (rank status value)
value::= phrase{(phrase(word supertag))}**

The final parse, a set of fully tagged predicate/argument structures, is then submitted into the generator that transforms every predicate/argument structure into a simple sentence. The generator determines the order of sentences, the order of words in the nascent sentences taking care of morphological forms and agreement. The order of the sentences follows the order of predicates in the claim. The order of the words in a sentence is defined by the knowledge in the PATTERNs zones of the predicate entries of the lexicon. Morphological synthesis and agreement are rule-based. The generic part and novelty parts of the claim are generated separately. The micro-level of simplification is illustrated in Figure 3.

5.4 Text-to-diagram simplification

Simplification of a claim text into a diagram is performed based of the internal claim representation as shown in Section 5.3. We here used the automatic text planner of the claim generator that was developed as a module of a patent MT system (Sheremetyeva, 2007).

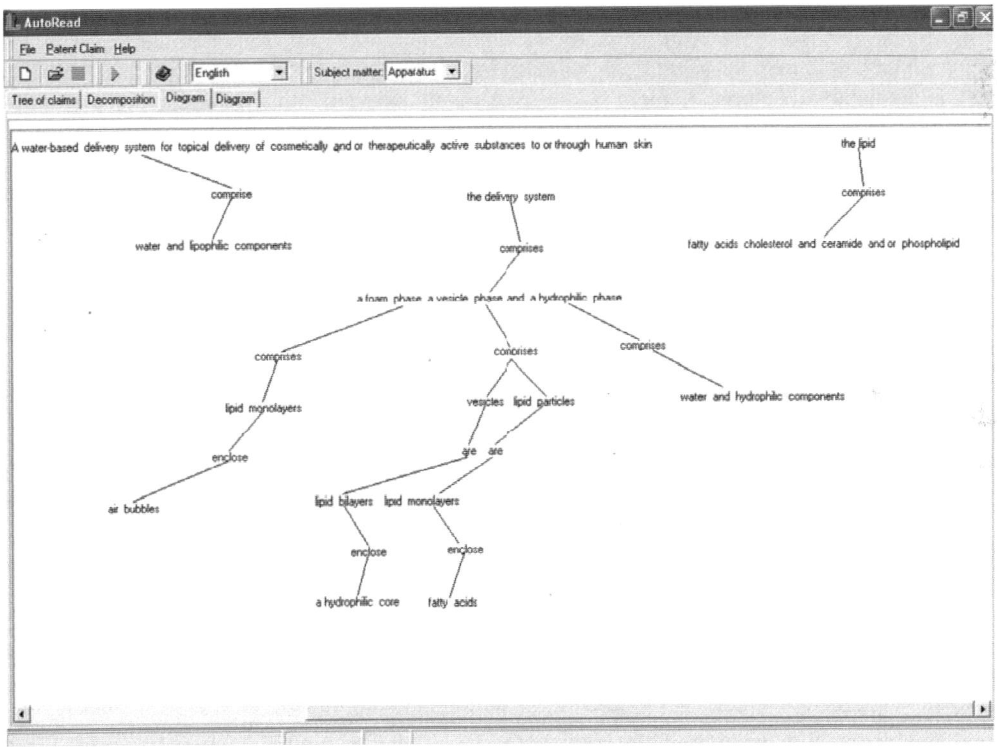

Figure 4. This screenshot of the "Diagram" page of the user interface which displays a conceptual schema of the invention underlying the claim text.

The planner runs over the output of the deep analyzer in the form of a set of separate predicate/argument structures and unifies separate predicate-argument structures into a hierarchical structure in the form of a single root tree or a forest of trees. The planning stage is guided by the constraints on the patent claim sublanguage. The unified trees of predicate structures are visualized for the reader in the form of a diagram with explicitly listed invention elements and their relations as in Figure 4.

6 Evaluation

Given that no reliable evaluation metrics exist so far for text simplification we performed a preliminary qualitative evaluation of our methodology based on human judgment (as in all cited works on claim simplification). Some of the researchers admit avoiding qualitative evaluation due to the lack of resources that would have made it possible (Mille and Wanner, 2008). The number of patents the authors use to evaluate their methodologies might seem quite limited, e.g., (Mille and Wanner, 2008) report evaluation results based on 30 patents; in (Bouayad-Agha et al.) the test corpus consisted of 29 patents; (Ferraro et al. 2014) inspected 38 patent documents, but again, the reason is the immense complexity and length of the patent claims.

There is no need to use readability formulas to prove the higher comprehensibility of the output of our macro- and micro level simplifiers as compared to the original claim section texts. These formulas are not applicable to the macro-level simplification. As for the micro-level simplification, the terminology of the original and simplified claims is kept unchanged and it is evident that simple and short sentences are "simpler" than long and complex ones.

We evaluate our methodology with a view to preserving the claim content and grammaticality as bad syntax can change the content of the claim with all the legal consequences. We asked human annotators (5 linguist students and 3 patent experts) to grade the simplification results according to these two criteria. The architecture of our system allows evaluating each component independently.

The quality evaluation method of nominal and predicate terminology extraction/highlighting consisted in comparing our results with a gold reference list. The gold lists of multi-component nominal terms and predicate terms were built manually by linguist students from the patent corpus of 72000 words for which it was feasible to create a gold standard. The number of multi-component NPs does not include the number of those NPs that only appear inside longer nominal phrases. The evaluation results of the extraction are in Table 1.

Table 1. Results of the extraction of nominal and predicate terminology

	Multicomponent NPs	Predicates
Total number of gold terms	1425	1272
Total extracted phrases	1476	1186
Correct terms	1394	1154
Missed terms	67	54
Incorrect phrases	24	-

Most of the missed NPs are longer than 4 words; they are missed because we limited ourselves to a 4-gram extraction model. The problem can be fixed by widening the extraction window which might increase the computation time. As for predicates, no incorrect terms were extracted because they were only searched against the predicate entries in the system lexicon in the "residue" of the claim text after NP extraction. Extraction mistakes can be corrected by updating the knowledge of the NP extractor.

The macro-level simplification (construction of the hierarchical trees of claims) was tested on 25 patents (each having from 7 to 98 claims of different kind). The performance at this level of simplification was practically perfect (i.e., for detecting the beginning and end of the claim section in a patent, the accuracy percentage is 100 and the trees of claims for every patent were also 100% correct. The result is explained by that the very shallow and closed knowledge required for this simplification procedure was completely covered in the lexicon.

Decomposition of a long claim sentence is undergoing extensive testing, further extension and knowledge update. It was feasible to test the methodology on the material of the first (most representative) claims of 25 patents containing from 5 to 10 predicates (meaning that claims should be decomposed into from 5 to 10 simple sentences, correspondingly). The total number of the resulting simple sentences is 147 out of which 93 sentences were correct. The problems are mainly due to the insufficient coverage of the rules identifying predicate/argument relations of syntactic chunks as output by the deep parser. However, these problems can be solved by the knowledge extension and brush-up. Already in their present state this simplifying component shows promising performance.

Building diagrams is performed by the planning component of a fully operational generator (see section 5.3). It is completely conditioned by the parser and correlates with the claim decomposition. Once the decomposition into simple sentences is correct, the diagram is correct as well.

7 Conclusions

In this paper, we have presented a methodology for the simplification of both the whole section of patent claims and individual claims. The simplification improves the readability of patent clams by the following: building a hierarchy of multiple claims with relevant accompanying information; highlighting the claim/patent nominal and predicate terminology; decomposing long and complex sentences of individual claims into a set of simple sentences preserving the content of the claim; building claim diagrams graphically visualizing interrelations of the invention elements.

Based on the methodology an experimental claim simplification tool was developed. As of today the programming shell of the tool is completed and provides for knowledge administration in all modules of the system to improve their performance. The static knowledge sources have been compiled for the domain of patents about apparatuses and chemical substances. The morphological analysis of English is fully operational and well tested. The English generator is also operational. The evaluation results suggest that our system produce much more readable output when compared to the original claims, and that the preservation of the claim content and grammaticality are positively rated by the annotators. The tool is currently undergoing an extensive extension and evaluation. However, already in it present state it provides for promising performance. The research is primarily targeted to patent experts, but can also be useful for laypeople and for automatic patent processing.

References

Aluisio S., Specia L., Gasperin C. and Scarton C. 2010. Readability assessment for text simplification. *Proceedings of the NAACL HLT 2010 Fifth Workshop on Innovative Use of NLP for Building Educational Applications*, pp.1–9.

Bott S., Saggion H. and Figueroa D. 2012. A Hybrid System for Spanish Text Simplification. *NAACL-HLT 2012 Workshop on Speech and Language Processing for Assistive Technologies (SLPAT),* pages 75–84, Montreal, Canada, June 7–8, 2012. c 2012 Association for Computational Linguistics

Bouayad-Agha N., Casamayor G.,Ferraro G., and Wanner L. 2009 Simplification of Patent ClaimSentences for Their Paraphrasing and Summarization. *Proceedings of the Twenty-Second International FLAIRS Conference.*

Brown, J. D. (1998). An EFL readability index. *JALT Journal*, 20, 7–36.

Crossley, S. A. & McNamara, D. S. 2008. Assessing Second Language Reading Texts at the Intermediate Level: An approximate replication of Crossley, Louwerse, McCarthy, and McNamara. *Language Teaching*, 41 (3), 409–229.

Crossley, S. A., Allen D. B. and McNamara D. S. 2011. Text readability and intuitive simplification: A comparison of readability formulas. *Reading in a Foreign Language*. April 2011, V. 23, No. 1. pp. 84–101

Dell'Orletta, F., Montemagni S., and Venturi G. 2011. READ–IT: Assessing Readability of Italian Texts with a View to Text Simplification. *Proceedings of the 2nd Workshop on Speech and Language Processing for Assistive Technologies,* Edinburgh, Scotland, UK, 2011, pp. 73-83.

Ferraro G., Suominen H., and Nualart J. 2014.Segmentation of patent claims for improving their readability *Proceedings of the 3rd Worshop on Predicting and Improving Text Readability for Target Reader Populations (PITR) @ EACL 2014*, pp. 66–73. Gothenburg, Sweden, April 26-30 2014. c 2014 Association for Computational Linguistics

Graesser, A. C., McNamara, D. D., Louwerse, M. L., and Cai, Z. 2004. Coh-Metrix: Analysis of text on cohesion and language. *Behavior Research Methods, Instruments, & Computers*, 36, 193–202.

Greenfield, J. (2004). Readability formulas for EFL. *JALT Journal*, 26, 5–24.

Mille S. and Wanner L. Multilingual Summarization in Practice: The Case of Patent Claims *12th EAMT conference,* 22-23 September 2008, Hamburg, Germany

Kincaid, J. P., Fishburne, R. P., Rogers, R. L. & Chissom, B. S. 1975. Derivation of new readability formulas (Automated Readability Index, Fog Count and Flesch Reading Ease Formula) for Navy enlisted personnel, *Research Branch Report 8–75, Millington, TN: Naval Technical Training,* U. S. Naval Air Station, Memphis,.

Petersen, S., and Ostendorf, M. 2007 Text simplification for language learners: a corpus analysis. *Proceedings of Workshop on Speech and Language Technology for Education*

Poornima C , Dhanalakshmi V, Anand Kumar M, and Soman K. P. 2011. Rule based Sentence Simplification for English to Tamil Machine Translation System. *International Journal of Computer Applications* (0975 – 8887) Volume 25– No.8, July 2011.

Pressman D. 2006. *Patent It Yourself.* Nolo, Berkeley, CA.

Rada D. V. 1995. Reading and understanding patent claims. *JOM*, 47(11):69–69.

Siddharthan, A. 2002. An Architecture for a Text Simplification System. *Proceedings of the Language Engineering Conference (LEC'02),* Hyderabad, India, IEEE Computer Society pp. 64.

Sheremetyeva S. 1999. A Flexible Approach To Multi-Lingual Knowledge Acquisition For NLG.. *Proceedings of the 7th European Workshop on Natural Language Generation.* Toulouse. (France) May 13-15.

Sheremetyeva S. 2003. Natural language analysis of patent claims. *Proceedings of the ACL 2003 Workshop on Patent Processing, ACL '03,* Stroudsburg, PA, USA. Association for Computational Linguistics.

Sheremetyeva S. 2007. On Portability of Resources for Quick Ramp-Up of Multilingual MT for Patent Claims. *Proceedings of the workshop on Patent Translation in conjunction with MT Summit XI,* Copenhagen, Denmark, September 10-14

Sheremetyeva S. 2009. On Extracting Multiword NP Terminology for MT. *Proceedings of the Thirteenth Conference of European Association of Machine Translation (EAMT-2009).* Barcelona, Spain. May 14-15.

Shinmori, A., Okumura M., Marukawa Y., and Iwayama M. (2003). Patent claim processing for readability: structure analysis and term explanation. *Proceedings of the ACL-2003 Workshop on Patent Corpus Processing, volume 20 of PATENT 03,* pp. 56–65, Stroudsburg, PA, USA. Association for Computational Linguistics.

Shinmori, A., Okumura M., Marukawa Y. 2012. Aligning patent claims with the"detailed description" for readability. *Journal of Natural Language Processing,* 12(3):111–128.

Takao D. and Sumita E. 2003. "Input sentence splitting and translation", *Proceedings of the Workshop on Building and using parallel Texts, HLT-NAACL 2003.*

Zhu, Z., Bernhard, D. and Gurevych, I. A. 2010. Monolingual Tree-based Translation Model for Sentence Simplification. *Proceedings of The 23rd International Conference on Computational Linguistics (COLING),* August 2010. Beijing, Chin.a

Making Biographical Data in Wikipedia Readable: A Pattern-based Multilingual Approach

Itziar Gonzalez-Dios, María Jesús Aranzabe, Arantza Díaz de Ilarraza
IXA NLP Group
University of the Basque Country (UPV/EHU)
itziar.gonzalezd@ehu.es

Abstract

In this paper we present *Biografix*, a pattern based tool that simplifies parenthetical structures with biographical information, whose aim is to create simple, readable and accessible sentences. To that end, we analysed the parenthetical structures that appear in the first paragraph of the Basque Wikipedia, and concentrated on biographies. Although it has been designed and developed for Basque we adapted it and evaluated with other five languages. We also perform an extrinsic evaluation with a question generation system to see if *Biografix* improve its results.

1 Introduction and motivation

Parentheticals are expressions, somehow structurally independent, that integrated in a text function as modifiers of phrases, sentences..., and add information or comments to the text. Therefore, it has been argued that they interrupt the prosodic flow, breaking the intonation. According to Dehé and Kavalova (2007), parentheticals can be realised in different ways: one-word parentheticals, sentence adverbials, comment clauses and reporting verbs, nominal apposition and non-restrictive relative clauses, question tags, clauses and backtracking. Besides, the authors argue that sometimes the parentheticals are not related to the host sentence neither semantically nor pragmatically, but they are understood in the text due to the situational context.

Some parentheticals can be the result of a stylistic choice (Blakemore, 2006) and that is the case of parenthetical information found in the first paragraph of some Wikipedia articles. As stated in the Wikipedia guidelines[1] the first paragraph of the articles should contain resuming and important information. That is why the information is there so condensed. Apart from condensing the information parentheticals cause long sentences, which are more difficult to process both for humans and for advanced applications. Moreover, web writting style books (Amatria et al., 2013) suggest not to use parenthetical constructs because they make more difficult the access to the information. Simple wikipedia guidelines[2] recommend also not to use two sets of brackets next to each other.

NLP applications such as question generation systems (QG) for educational domain[3] may fail when finding important information in brackets. For example, if we want to create questions, systems such as the presented in Aldabe et al. (2013) will look for a verb[4]. In the case of parenthetical biographical information there is no verb which makes explicit when the person is born or when she or he died. So, no question will be created based on that information.

The study of parentheticals in Basque has been limited to the analysis of the irony in the narrativity of Koldo Mitxelena (Azpeitia, 2011). In the present study we analyse the parentheticals that are used in the first paragraph of the Basque Wikipedia and developed a rule-based tool *Biografix* to detect these

[1] http://en.wikipedia.org/wiki/Wikipedia:Manual_of_Style (last accessed: March, 2014)

[2] http://simple.wikipedia.org/wiki/Wikipedia:Manual_of_Style (last accessed: March, 2014)

[3] Question generation is important in learning technologies (intelligent tutoring systems, inquiry-based environments, and game-based learning environments), virtual environments and dialogue systems among others. http://www.questiongeneration.org/ (last accessed: April, 2014)

[4] Both systems (one chunk-based and another dependency-based) presented in Aldabe et al. (2013) follow the guidelines presented in Rus and Graesser (2009).

structures and to create new sentences out of them. To be more concrete, we concentrate on biographical information since there are not explicit words in text that give a clue about what type of information it is. Our aim is to make more readable sentences and, consequently, to eliminate the interruption they cause. About the domain of biographies, their automatic generation has been studied (Duboue et al., 2003) in Natural Language Generation (NLG). In this research line, referring expressions to people have been studied for automatic summarisation of news (Siddharthan et al., 2011). The quality of the biographies (linguistic and content) has been recently analysed in the English Wikipedia (Flekova et al., 2014).

We want also to make a first step towards the simplification of Basque Wikipedia, since English simple wikipedia has been a great resource for Text Simplification (TS) and Readability Assessement (RA). Efforts for simple wikipedia have also been made for Portuguese (Junior et al., 2011) using TS techniques. Although *Biografix* has been specially developed for Basque, being pattern-based, we have also evaluated its adaptation to other languages. This work is not limited to wikipedia, *Biografix* can be used on other types of text as well, since these structures can be found in educational texts, newspapers and so on.

This paper is structured as follows: after this introduction we report in section 2 the treatment of parentheticals in TS and in Wikipedia. In section 3 we describe *Biografix* and in section 4 we report its evaluation. Finally, we conclude and outline the future work in section 5.

2 Parenthetical Structures

In this section we report the treatment that parenthentical structures have undergone in TS and other NLP applications. We also describe the parentheticals found in Basque Wikipedia.

Parentheticals have been object of study in TS and three main operations have been proposed: a) parentheticals have been removed out of the texts (Drndarević et al., 2013), b) parentheticals have been removed but they have been kept in another form (Aranzabe et al., 2012; Seretan, 2012) or c) parentheticals have been added to explain the meaning by short paraphrases (Hallett and Hardcastle, 2008) or hyperonyms (Leroy et al., 2013). In any case, it is usually recommended to avoid them (Aluísio et al., 2008). In other NLP applications such as summarisation they are usually removed and even some QG works follow the same strategy, in case they are not relevant (Heilman and Smith, 2010).

2.1 Parenthetical Structures in Basque Wikipedia

Wikipedia guidelines emphasise the importance of the first paragraph. It should indeed contain a summary of the most significant information. To concentrate all the information, stylistic resources such as parenthentical structures are used. The information that is written in brackets in the Basque Wikipedia can be classified in two groups: a) information about people and b) information about concepts. About people biographical data and mandates are usually found and about concepts the etymology of words is frequent. Translations or transliterations of the named entity or the concept is found for both groups.

On the other hand, there are other frequent parenthetical structures that are found in the first paragraph, but they are not written in brackets. This is the case of the nicknames, which are written in commas. This kind of information is also found in other languages. After this analysis, we decided to concentrate on biographical data to create new sentences out of that information.

Biographical data Contrary to English Wikipedia, in Basque Wikipedia the information contained in bracket is, if known, birthplace (town, province, state), date of birth, and if the person is dead, date of death and place of dead. This is the case as well of the Catalan, Spanish, Italian, Portuguese, German and French Wikipedia among others, although sometimes paraphrases are found in brackets. For French there is, for example, more than a way to write the biographical data[5].

In Basque Wikipedia guidelines[6] it is stated that biographical data should be written as in examples 1 and 2. If the person is dead, we see in example 1 that the birth data (town, state and date) and the death data (town, state and date) are linked by a dash.

[5] `http://fr.wikipedia.org/wiki/Wikipedia:Conventions_de_style` (last accessed: March, 2014)
[6] `http://eu.wikipedia.org/wiki/Wikipedia:Artikuluen_formatua` (last accessed: March, 2014)

(1) *Ernest Rutherford, Nelsongo lehenengo baroia, (Brightwater, Zeelanda Berria, 1871ko abuztuaren 30a - Cambridge, Ingalaterra, 1937ko urriaren 19a) fisika nuklearraren aita izan zen.*
'Ernest Rutherford, 1st Baron Rutherford of Nelson, (Brightwater, New Zeeland, 30th August, 1871 - Cambridge, England, 19th October, 1937) was the father of the nuclear Physics.'

And if the person is alive, only birth data (town, province, date) is provided as in example 2.

(2) *Karlos Argiñano Urkiola, nazioartean Karlos Arguiñano grafiaz ezagunagoa, (Beasain, Gipuzkoa, 1948ko irailaren 6a) sukaldari, aktore eta enpresaburu euskalduna da.*
'Karlos Argiñano Urkiola, internationally known with the Karlos Arguiñano spelling, (Beasain, Gipuzkoa, 6th September, 1948) is a basque chef, actor and businessman.'

In both cases, the places (if known) should precede the date and these should be separated by commas. However, biographical data is not frequently written uniformly. Places do not precede the date, the date is incomplete (only year) and sometimes other characters like the question mark appear to denote that the place or the date is known.

Taking into account this guidelines and the articles we have analysed, we have developed *Biografix*, a pattern based tool that detects biographical data and creates new sentences with this information. This tool was originally developed for Basque but it has been adapted to other languages. An adaptation of this tool, moreover, could be used as a first step into Text Summarisation, if we only remove the parentheticals and do not create new sentences.

Biographical information is contained in brackets in other Wikipedias as well but formats may be different. The way of writing, for example, in Catalan, German and Portuguese is similar to Basque. In Spanish, French, and Italian that format is also used but, as mentioned beforehand, other formats are also accepted.

3 Inside *Biografix*

Biografix is a pattern-based tool that simplifies the biographical data and creates new sentences out of that information. Having as an input the example 1 in subsection 2.1, *Biografix* will produce the sentences 3, 4, 5, 6 and 7.

(3) *Ernest Rutherford, Nelsongo lehenengo baroia, fisika nuklearraren aita izan zen.*
'Ernest Rutherford, 1st Baron Rutherford of Nelson, was the father of the nuclear Physics.'

(4) *Ernest Rutherford 1871ko abuztuaren 30ean Brightwateren jaio zen.*
'Ernest Rutherford was born on the 30th of August, 1871 in Brightwater.'

(5) *Brightwater Zeelanda Berrian dago.*
'Brightwater is in New Zeeland.'

(6) *Ernest Rutherford 1937ko urriaren 19an Cambridgen hil zen.*
'Ernest Rutherford died on the 19th of October, 1937 in Cambridge.'

(7) *Cambridge Ingalaterran dago.*
'Cambridge is in England.'

So, if the person is dead, *Biografix* will write first the main sentence (3) followed by a new sentence (4) with the information about the birth. If the birthplace is composed by more than a place entity, sentences like (5) will be written. After the birth information, a sentence will contain the information about the death (6). For the cases that more than a place appear, those will be rewritten (7).

If the person is alive like in example 2 in subsection 2.1, the same process will take place, but no death information will appear by creating the new sentences 8, 9 and 10.

(8) *Karlos Argiñano Urkiola, nazioartean Karlos Arguiñano grafiaz ezagunagoa, sukaldari, aktore eta enpresaburu euskalduna da.*
'Karlos Argiñano Urkiola, internationally known with the Karlos Arguiñano spelling, is a basque chef, actor and businessman.'

(9) *Karlos Argiñano 1948ko irailaren 6an Beasainen jaio zen.*
'Karlos Argiñano was born on the 6th of September, 1948 in Beasain.'

(10) *Beasain Gipuzkoan dago.*
'Beasain is in Gipuzkoa.'

So, first, main information will be kept (8) and then the information about the birth will appear (9). As a second place information (the province) original sentence (2), it will be rewritten as well (10).

We have to mention that we use the title of the article as the subject of the sentences containing the biographical information. That is way we see that in sentences 9 and 10 the subject is *Karlos Argiñano* and the subject in sentence 8 is *Karlos Argiñano Urkiola*. We took this decision for cases where the real name of person is not so known, e.g. Cherilyn Sarkisian. Had we used Cherilyn Sarkisian in all the sentences, would someone have known we are talking about Cher?

To carry out these simplifying transformations *Biografix* follows the simplification process explained in Aranzabe et al. (2012):

- **Splitting:** In this stage we get the parts of the sentences we are going to work with. To that end, three steps take place: a) the parenthetical structure is removed from the original sentence; b) the type of parenthetical expression is checked looking at whether there are birth and death data or only the former; c) dates and places are split. We use simple patterns to detect the dates and the places. As it is possible to find more than a place, they will be split by the commas. This stage is common for all the languages.

- **Reconstruction:** The new simplified sentences are created in this stage. This part is language-dependent, since we add the verbs, determinants, prepositions and case markers. In the case of Basque we also remove the absolutive case that is found in some articles[7]. Anyway, we create three kind of sentences that are common for all the languages with the constructs obtained in the splitting stage: a) sentences indicating birth data, b) sentences indicating death data and c) sentences indicating place specifications. The main sentence will be kept as in the original version (the parenthetical has been removed in the splitting stage).

- **Reordering:** The sentences will be ordered in text. First, the main sentence; second, the information about the birth; if there is more than a place, the following sentences will contain that information (place specifications); third, the information about the death (if dead) and finally, the death place specifications.

- **Correction:** The aim of this stage is to check if there are any mistake in the new sentences and to correct them. As one of our goals is to know the correctness of *Biografix*'s output this stage has not been implemented yet.

Biografix has been designed for Basque and then the reconstruction stage has been adapted to other 7 languages: French, German, Spanish, Catalan, Galician, Italian and Portuguese. To develop the Basque version we implemented the guidelines in Wikipedia (see subsection 2.1) and we used a small corpus of 50 sentences to find possible cases, where the guidelines are not fulfilled. These 50 sentences were randomly crawled.

For other languages, we did not make any change in the splitting stage but for German. According to German Wikipedia guidelines birth and death data are separated by a semicolon and not by a dash. Although French, Spanish and Italian have other options to express the biographical information between bracket we did not implement them. Our aim is not to create a tool specially for these languages, but to see if the design for Basque can be applicable to other languages. That is why, the adaptations to other languages are available at our website[8], if someone wants to improve them.

[7]The absolutive case is used according to the format of the date.
[8]`https://ixa.si.ehu.es/Ixa/Produktuak/1403535629`

Other improvements could be done in the reconstruction stage. To rewrite the sentences we have used the most familiar past tense in each language. The only exception was French. The most familiar past tense according to the context is the *passé composé* but this tense requires the agreement of the gender between subject and verb[9]. As the *passé simple* is not very familiar we decided to use the present tense to avoid the concordance problem. So, this could be one of the things to take into account for future developers.

No other changes should be done in the reordering stage but the correction has to be adapted to each language. No training was performed for the other languages. Only 3-5 sentences were used to check that there were no errors.

4 Evaluation

In order to evaluate *Biografix* we crawled the first sentence of 30 Wikipedia articles. The method to select these articles was the following: a) we used CatScan V2.0β[10] to get a list of the Biographies in Basque Wikipedia; b) we randomised that list and make another list to see which articles were written in 8 languages (Basque, Catalan, French, Galician, German, Italian, Portuguese and Spanish); c) we selected the first 32 articles. The first two articles were used to explain and train the annotators. The final test-sample had, therefore, 30 items.

Having that sample, we performed two evaluations: a manual evaluation (section 4.1) and a extrinsic evaluation with a question generation system (section 4.2).

4.1 Manual evaluation

The manual evaluation was carried out for 6 languages: Basque, Catalan, French, Galician, German and Spanish. 10 linguists took part in the evaluation process and they evaluated three aspects of the task: the original sentences (*JatTestua*), *Biografix* performance (*Prog*) and the grammaticality of the new simplified sentences (*Gram*). In total they answered nine yes/no questions. This evaluation method we are proposing is useful to perform an error analysis and find out which are the weak points of our tool.

To evaluate the performance and the adaptation of *Biografix* we chose six languages according to the format of the biographical data: i) Basque (the language *Biografix* has been designed for) ii) Catalan (same format as Basque), iii) German (same format but a slightly variation), iv) Spanish (same format as Basque but other options as well), v) French (same format as Basque in one of the parenthetical formats and other options), vi) Galician (without defined format). Portuguese and Italian were not evaluated because their case studies were already evaluated with Catalan and Spanish. All the sample were evaluated by two annotators except for Catalan and Galician, because Catalan has the same case study as Basque and Galician has not a predefined format that could cause confusion.

Questions concerning the original sentences (*JatTestua*) Three questions were presented in regards to the original sentence in Wikipedia. The aim is to know if the original sentences do have parenthetical structures and therefore, how many of them are candidates to simplification (coverage).

1. Are there parenthetical structures written between brackets?

2. Is the sentence grammatically correct and standard?

3. Is the punctuation correct?

We asked about the grammaticality and the punctuation of original sentences (correctness) because it was shown in Aldabe et al. (2013) that many source sentences were incorrect and that fact decreased the performance of the question generators and the correctness of the created questions.

[9]e.g. *Cher est née en Californie.*, but *Ernest Rutherford est néø en Angleterre.*

[10]`http://tools.wmflabs.org/catscan2/catscan2.php` (last accessed: March, 2014)

Questions concerning the performance of *Biografix* (*Prog*) Four questions were designed to check if *Biografix* carries out the process it has been implemented for (precision).

1. Have parenthetical structures been removed?
2. Is all the information kept?
3. Taking into account the original sentence, is all the information correct?
4. Is there new information?

Second and third questions are essential to know if at rewriting in the reconstruction stage no information has been omitted or changed. The aim of the forth question is to know, for example, if sentences with other kind of information like translations have been added and treated as biographical or if a sentence referring to the death of a living person has been created.

Questions concerning the grammaticality of the new simplified sentences (*Gram*) Two questions were prepared to check the correctness of the simplified questions, since to create correct sentences is very important to understand the text. These questions should be answered for each simplified sentence (grammatical precision).

1. Is the sentence grammatically correct and standard?
2. Is the punctuation correct?

If these questions get negative results, we cannot forget that in our simplification study we consider the correction as a last step. This way, the output of *Biografix* will be checked and, were there any mistakes, they would be corrected.

4.1.1 Results of the manual evaluation

In table 1 we present the results obtained in the manual evaluation and it shows the results considering the following measures:

1. The coverage is the percentages out of 30 (the size of the sample) *Biografix* processed, that is, the sentences that had parentheticals.
2. The correctness is the percentage of the source sentences whose grammar and punctuation is correct.
3. The recall is the division between the number of the created simple sentences and the number of the sentences it should have created taking into account all the information in the original sentences.
4. The precision is the division between the correct performed, that is, all the *Prog* questions have been correctly answered and the processed sentences. We call this precision at performance.
5. The grammatical precision is the correctly created sentences among the created sentences.

In the second-last column we show the κ agreement of the evaluators (Cohen, 1960). As we have few examples, the expected agreement is very high and it causes low scores. That is the reason why we also show the percentage agreement (observed agreement) in the last column.

Taking a look at the results for Basque, we see that Biografix is able to create almost all the sentences (recall: 0.94) and that they are correct (grammatical precision: 0.87), although there are little problems keeping all the information and keeping it right (precision: 0.79). Taking into account that the percentage of the correct source sentences is low (82.76), we follow Aldabe et al. (2013) and recalculate the results without the incorrect sentences. This way, recall is 0.93, precision is 0.80, grammatical precision is 0.88. As we see, results do not vary that much, since the grammaticality of the source sentence has only influence in the first of the created sentences. About the agreement between annotators, we see that κ is really low (0.37) due to the few disagreements that annotators had above all about the grammar. However, the observed agreement is high (90.63).

Language	Coverage	Correctness	Recall	Precision	Gram. Prec.	κ	%
Basque	97.00	82.76	0.94	0.79	0.87	0.37	90.63
Catalan	93.33	98.21	0.77	0.53	0.78	-	-
French	73.00	88.64	0.80	0.18	0.37	0.39	85.06
Galician	43.00	88.46	0.76	0.15	0.62	-	-
German	100	100.00	0.78	0.60	0.78	-	100
Spanish	100	85.00	0.71	0.33	0.67	0.52	88.76

Table 1: Results of *Biografix* language by language

In the case of Catalan, we see that *Biografix* is not able to create as many sentences as information in the original source (recall: 0.77) and this tendency occurs in the other languages as well. Precision at performance goes down (0.53) due to added and lost information but grammatical precision is acceptable (0.78). We think, that this is a quite satisfactory adaptation.

The results for French indicate that something went wrong. There is more than a way to express the biographical information and, as expected, the performance goes down. The precision is very low (0.18) due to the fact that a lot of information is lost and as sometime paraphrases do appear in the original sentence, this fact implies grammatical error. Anyhow, the recall is acceptable (0.80) and that is a good starting point for the further development of French version. The average of the obtained κ measures is really low (0.39) and that is why having few instances Cohen's kappa penalises the disagreement too much.

The case of Galician is quite different. It is not stated in the guidelines how biographical data should be written and the parentheticals we found are few (coverage: 43.00) and different from the Basque. However, we wanted to try *Biografix* and what we see is, that, although its precision at performance is really low (0.15), the created sentences are quite correct (0.62). We think the Galician Wikipedia should be analysed thoroughly and then *Biografix* should be adjusted.

The German version of *Biografix* was able to simplify all the sentences found in the test-sample and its recall is high (0.88). Its weak point is the precision at performance (0.60), as in other languages, due to the fact that the second question of *Prog* is not satisfied. The sentence it creates are quite acceptable (0.71) as well. Surprisingly, both linguists agreed in all the cases and questions. So, we conclude that the German adaptation was successful.

Finally, in the case of the Spanish adaptation, we see that the precision is very low (0.33) since there was an important information loss. However, the grammatical precision (0.67) is acceptable. Although κ is higher (0.52) than in other languages, observed agreement is not far from Basque (88.76). It is remarkable as well that being Spanish a long time normalised language only the 85.00 % of the source sentence are correct and that although there are other formats to express the biographical information the coverage is absolute (100.00).

The main disagreement was found when evaluating the grammar and the punctuation due to different criteria of the annotators. For some of them sentences without verb were correct because they considered that there was an elided verb. In our opinion, as we are trying to simplify, we think that all the sentences should have a finite verb. Annotators did not have to much trouble to answer the four *Prog* questions, so we think that this is a good methodology, and, moreover, it makes easy to perform error analysis. We want to point out that κ has not been the best measure but we have used it as we consider that it is a standard to measure data reliability.

To conclude, we find that there is room to improve the versions in other languages, above all trying not to lose information but the adaptation of *Biografix* has been a good starting point. In fact, the adaptation has been quite satisfactory for German and Catalan, because they share the format with Basque but they should be further analysed. As foreseen, the languages with different formats like Galician, Spanish and French require a bigger analysis.

4.2 Extrinsic evaluation

To evaluate the performance of *Biografix* throughout another NLP advanced application, we used the web application *Seneko* (Lopez-Gazpio and Maritxalar, 2013)[11], the application of the chunk-based question generation system for educational purposes presented in Aldabe et al. (2013). This kind of evaluation was only performed for Basque.

We ran *Seneko* with the original sentences and the simplified sentences. The number of the generated questions is presented in table 2. We break down the results on the basis of the case markers as well. In agglutinative languages like Basque case markers are the morphemes that express the grammatical functions.

Source file	Total	Absolutive	Inessive	Genitive	Other
Original sentences	34	23	7	2	2
Simplified sentences	142	65	66	8	3

Table 2: Questions generated by *Seneko* using the original and the simplified sentences

Using as input the original sentences *Seneko* is able to create 34 questions, more or less a question per sentence. 23 of them have been generated for the absolutive case, that is, for the subject and the predicative, and only 7 of them have been generated for the inessive. Taking into account that we are working with biographical information, this is a bad result because the inessive case in Basque is used to express time and place relations. That is, the inessive is used to create questions with the question words *When* and *Where*. On the other hand, using as source the simplified sentences, 65 questions have been generated for the absolutive and 66 for the inessive. This way, we see that using *Biografix*'s output *Seneko* has been able to generate questions about place and time expressions.

Next, in 11 and 12 we show an example of the questions generated by *Seneko*. In 11 we find that using the original input it was only able to create a question, and it makes no sense but using the simplified text (example 12) *Seneko* creates two correct questions.

(11) a. **Source text:** *Eduardo Hughes Galeano (Montevideo, 1940ko irailaren 3a -) Uruguaiko kazetari eta idazlea da.*
'Eduardo Hughes Galeano (Montevideo, 3rd of September, 1940 -) is an Uruguayan journalist and writer.'

b. **Generated question:** *Nor da Eduardo Hughes Galeano Montevideo 1940ko irailaren 3a?*
'Who is Eduardo Hughes Galeano Montevideo 3rd of September, 1940?'

(12) a. **Simplified text:** *Eduardo Hughes Galeano Uruguaiko kazetari eta idazlea da. Eduardo Galeano 1940ko irailaren 3an Montevideon jaio zen.*
'Eduardo Hughes Galeano is an Uruguayan journalist and writer. Eduardo Hughes Galeano was born the 3rd of September, 1940 in Montevideo.'

b. **Generated questions:** *Nor jaio zen 1940ko irailaren 3an Montevideon? Non jaio zen Eduardo Galeano 1940ko irailaren 3an?*
'Who was born on the 3rd of September, 1940 in Montevideo? Where was born Eduardo Hughes Galeano on the 3rd of September, 1940?'

This way, we conclude that *Biografix* is an useful tool to improve the performance of question generation systems like *Seneko*.

5 Conclusion and future work

In this paper we have presented *Biografix*, a tool that detects parenthetical structures and simplifies the biographical data in order to create new more readable sentences. Although *Biografix* has been

[11] `http://ixa2.si.ehu.es/seneko/` (last accessed: March, 2014)

designed and developed for Basque, we have applied it to the parenthetical biographical information written in other seven languages: French, German, Spanish, Catalan, Galician, Italian and Portuguese. The results of the evaluation show that the Basque version obtains very good results but the adaptations should be further developed. Anyway, good results have been obtained for Catalan and German and promising for Spanish and French. Besides, we have shown its validity through an extrinsic evaluation with *Seneko*, a question generation system. These systems are important for the educational domain, and the improvement *Biografix* offers is considerable. Although we have used Wikipedia to develop and evaluate *Biografix*, it can be used for other kind of text with parenthetical biographical information.

For the future, we plan to continue analysing and implementing rules for other kind of parenthetical structures like etymology, translations of named entities or mandates of relevant people. We also plan to link the entities to the their articles in Wikipedia to offer additional information. Patterns could also be improved using previously developed analysers or tools, but this way the splitting stage will become language-dependent. Moreover, we cannot forget that this work is included in the main framework of the TS system for Basque that we are developing and this is another step towards the main aim of getting easier and more readable Basque texts.

Acknowledgements

Itziar Gonzalez-Dios's work is funded by a PhD grant from the Basque Government. We thank Aitor Soroa for his help with the language links in Wikipedia. A great part of this work would have not been able without the collaboration of the linguists Itziar Aduriz, Izaskun Aldezabal, Begoña Altuna, Nora Aranberri, Klara Ceberio, Ainara Estarrona, Mikel Iruskieta, Mikel Lersundi and Uxoa Iñurrieta. We also do appreciate the help Ander Soraluze offered during the implementation of *Biografix* and Oier Lopez de Lacalle for his quick tutorial on R. This research was supported by the Basque Government (IT344-10), and the Spanish Ministry of Science and Innovation, Hibrido Sint project (MICINN, TIN2010-202181).

References

Itziar Aldabe, Itziar Gonzalez-Dios, Iñigo Lopez-Gazpio, Ion Madrazo, and Montse Maritxalar. 2013. Two Approaches to Generate Questions in Basque. *Procesamiento del Lenguaje Natural*, 51:101–108.

Sandra M. Aluísio, Lucia Specia, Thiago A. S. Pardo, Erick G. Maziero, Helena M. Caseli, and Renata P. M. Fortes. 2008. A corpus analysis of simple account texts and the proposal of simplification strategies: first steps towards text simplification systems. In *Proceedings of the 26th annual ACM international conference on Design of communication*, SIGDOC '08, pages 15–22, New York, NY, USA. ACM.

Xabier Amatria, Urtzi Barrenetxea, Irene Fernández, Rakel Olea, Joseba Uskola, and Izaskun Zuntzunegi. 2013. *Komunikazio elektronikoa. IVAPen gomendioak web-orriak idazteko*. IVAP.

María Jesús Aranzabe, Arantza Díaz de Ilarraza, and Itziar Gonzalez-Dios. 2012. First Approach to Automatic Text Simplification in Basque. In Luz Rello and Horacio Saggion, editors, *Proceedings of the Natural Language Processing for Improving Textual Accessibility (NLP4ITA) workshop (LREC 2012)*, pages 1–8.

Agurtzane Azpeitia. 2011. Enuntziatu parentetikoak: Koldo Mitxelenaren intentzio ironikoaren ispilu. *Gogoa*, 10(1&2).

Diane Blakemore. 2006. Divisions of labour: The analysis of parentheticals. *Lingua*, 116(10):1670–1687. Language in Mind: A Tribute to Neil Smith on the Occasion of his Retirement.

Jacob Cohen. 1960. A Coefficient of Agreement for Nominal Scales. *Educational and Psychological Measurement*, 20:37–46.

Nicole Dehé and Yordanka Kavalova. 2007. Parentheticals. An introduction. In Nicole Dehé and Yordanka Kavalova, editors, *Parentheticals*, pages 1–22. John Benjamins Publishing Company.

Biljana Drndarević, Sanja Štajner, Stefan Bott, Susana Bautista, and Horacio Saggion. 2013. Automatic Text Simplification in Spanish: A Comparative Evaluation of Complementing Modules. In *Computational Linguistics and Intelligent Text Processing*, pages 488–500. Springer.

Pablo A. Duboue, Kathleen R. McKeown, and Vasileios Hatzivassiloglou. 2003. PROGENIE: Biographical Descriptions for Intelligence Analysis. In *Proceedings of the 1st NSF/NIJ Conference on Intelligence and Security Informatics*, ISI'03, pages 343–345, Berlin, Heidelberg. Springer-Verlag.

Lucie Flekova, Oliver Ferschke, and Iryna Gurevych. 2014. What Makes a Good Biography?: Multidimensional Quality Analysis Based on Wikipedia Article Feedback Data. In *Proceedings of the 23rd International Conference on World Wide Web*, WWW '14, pages 855–866, Republic and Canton of Geneva, Switzerland. International World Wide Web Conferences Steering Committee.

Catalina Hallett and David Hardcastle. 2008. Automatic Rewriting of Patient Record Narratives. In Nicoletta Calzolari (Conference Chair), Khalid Choukri, Joseph Maegaard, Benteand Mariani, Jan Odijk, Stelios Piperidis, and Daniel Tapias, editors, *Proceedings of the Sixth International Conference on Language Resources and Evaluation (LREC'08)*, Marrakech, Morocco, May. European Language Resources Association (ELRA).

Michael Heilman and Noah A Smith. 2010. Extracting Simplified Statements for Factual Question Generation. In *Proceedings of QG2010: The Third Workshop on Ques-tion Generation*, page 11.

Arnaldo Candido Junior, Ann Copestake, Lucia Specia, and Sandra Maria Aluísio. 2011. Towards an on-demand simple portuguese wikipedia. In *Proceedings of the Second Workshop on Speech and Language Processing for Assistive Technologies*, pages 137–147. Association for Computational Linguistics.

Gondy Leroy, David Kauchak, and Obay Mouradi. 2013. A user-study measuring the effects of lexical simplification and coherence enhancement on perceived and actual text difficulty. *International Journal of Medical Informatics*, 82(8):717–730.

Iñigo Lopez-Gazpio and Montse Maritxalar. 2013. Web application for Reading Practice. In IADAT, editor, *IADAT-e2013: Proceedings of the 6th IADAT International Conference on Education*, pages 74–78.

Vasile Rus and Arthur C. Graesser. 2009. The Question Generation Shared Task and Evaluation Challenge. In *The University of Memphis. National Science Foundation.*

Violeta Seretan. 2012. Acquisition of Syntactic Simplification Rules for French. In Nicoletta Calzolari (Conference Chair), Khalid Choukri, Thierry Declerck, Mehmet Uur Doan, Bente Maegaard, Joseph Mariani, Jan Odijk, and Stelios Piperidis, editors, *Proceedings of the Eight International Conference on Language Resources and Evaluation (LREC'12)*, Istanbul, Turkey, May. European Language Resources Association (ELRA).

Advaith Siddharthan, Ani Nenkova, and Kathleen McKeown. 2011. Information Status Distinctions and Referring Expressions: An Empirical Study of References to People in News Summaries. *Comput. Linguist.*, 37(4):811–842, December.

Assessing Conformance of Manually Simplified Corpora with User Requirements: the Case of Autistic Readers

Sanja Štajner and **Richard Evans** and **Iustin Dornescu**
Research Group in Computational Linguistics
Research Institute of Information and Language Processing
University of Wolverhampton, UK
{SanjaStajner, R.J.Evans, I.Dornescu2}@wlv.ac.uk

Abstract

In the state of the art, there are scarce resources available to support development and evaluation of automatic text simplification (TS) systems for specific target populations. These comprise parallel corpora consisting of texts in their original form and in a form that is more accessible for different categories of target reader, including neurotypical second language learners and young readers. In this paper, we investigate the potential to exploit resources developed for such readers to support the development of a text simplification system for use by people with autistic spectrum disorders (ASD). We analysed four corpora in terms of nineteen linguistic features which pose obstacles to reading comprehension for people with ASD. The results indicate that the Britannica TS parallel corpus (aimed at young readers) and the Weekly Reader TS parallel corpus (aimed at second language learners) may be suitable for training a TS system to assist people with ASD. Two sets of classification experiments intended to discriminate between original and simplified texts according to the nineteen features lent further support for those findings.

1 Introduction

As a fundamental human right, people with reading and comprehension difficulties are entitled to access written information (UN, 2006). This entitlement enables better inclusion into society. However, the vast majority of texts that such people encounter in their everyday life – especially newswire texts – are lexically and syntactically very complex. Since the late nineties, several initiatives have emerged which propose guidelines for producing plain, easy-to-read and more accessible documents. These include the "Federal Plain Language Guidelines"[1], "Make it Simple, European Guidelines for the Production of Easy-to-Read Information for people with Learning Disability" (Freyhoff et al., 1998), "Am I making myself clear? Mencap's guidelines for accessible writing"[2], and the W3C – Web Accessibility Initiative guidelines[3]. However, manual adaptation of texts cannot match the speed with which new texts are published on the web in order to provide up to date information. The aim of Automatic Text Simplification (ATS) is to automatically (or at least semi-automatically) convert complex sentences into a more accessible form while preserving their original meaning. In the last twenty years, many ATS systems have been proposed for different target populations in various languages (Carroll et al., 1998; Devlin and Unthank, 2006; Saggion et al., 2011; Inui et al., 2003; Aluísio et al., 2008). Due to the scarcity of parallel corpora of original and manually simplified texts, most of these systems are rule-based.

The emergence of Simple English Wikipedia (SEW)[4], together with the existing English Wikipedia (EW)[5] provided a large amount of parallel TS training data, which motivated a shift in English TS from rule-based to data-driven approaches (Yatskar et al., 2010; Biran et al., 2011; Woodsend and Lapata, 2011; Coster and Kauchak, 2011; Wubben et al., 2012; Zhu et al., 2010). However, no assessment has

[1]http://www.plainlanguage.gov/howto/guidelines/bigdoc/fullbigdoc.pdf

[2]http://www.easy-read-online.co.uk/media/10609/making-myself-clear.pdf

[3]http://www.w3.org/WAI/

[4]http://simple.wikipedia.org/wiki/Main_Page

[5]http://wikipedia.org/wiki/Main_Page

ever been made of the quality of the simplifications made in SEW and the usefulness of the transformations learned from EW–SEW parallel corpora for any of the specified target populations. The only instructions given to the authors of SEW are to use Basic English vocabulary and shorter sentences. The main page states that SEW is for everyone, including children and adults who are learning English. All previously mentioned studies conducted on that corpus evaluated the quality of the generated output in terms of grammaticality, meaning preservation, and simplicity, but not usefulness. Also, there have been no comparisons of the types of transformations present in EW–SEW with any of the other TS corpora in English which were simplified with a specific target population in mind, e.g. Encyclopedia Britannica and its manually simplified versions for children – Britannica Elementary (Barzilay and Elhadad, 2003)[6], Guardian Weekly and its manually simplified versions for language learners (Allen, 2009), and the FIRST corpus of various texts simplified for people with autism spectrum disorder (ASD)[7].

In this study, we compare the original and simplified texts of the four aforementioned TS corpora in terms of nineteen features which measure the complexity of texts for people with ASD. Although these features were derived from user requirements for people with ASD, many of them are known to present reading obstacles for other target populations as well (e.g. children or language learners). Given the lack of parallel TS corpora for people with ASD, our main goal is to investigate whether the EW–SEW or the other two corpora aimed at children and language learners could be used as training material for a TS system to assist people with ASD and thus enable data-driven approaches (instead of the currently used rule-based ones). In order to further support the results of this analysis, we conduct several classification experiments in which we try to distinguish between original and simplified texts in each of the four corpora, using the nineteen features.

2 The FIRST Project and User Requirements

Autistic Spectrum Disorders (ASD) are neurodevelopmental disorders characterised by qualitative impairment in communication and stereotyped repetitive behaviour. People with ASD show a diverse range of reading abilities: 5-10% have the capacity to read words from an early age without the need for formal learning (hyperlexia) but many demonstrate reduced comprehension of what has been read (Volkmar and Wiesner, 2009). They may have difficulty inferring contextual information or may have trouble understanding mental verbs, emotional language, and long sentences with complex syntactic structure (Tager-Flusberg, 1981; Kover et al., 2012). To address these difficulties, a tool is being developed in the FIRST project[8] to assist in the process of making texts more accessible for people with ASD. To achieve this, three modues are exploited:

1. **Structural complexity processor**, which detects syntactically complex sentences and generates alternatives to such sentences in the form of sequences of shorter sentences (Evans et al., 2014; Dornescu et al., 2013).
2. **Meaning disambiguator**, which resolves pronominal references, performs word sense disambiguation, and detects lexicalised (conventional) metaphors (Barbu et al., 2013).
3. **Personalised document generator**, which aggregates the output of processors 1 and 2 and generates additional elements such as glossaries, illustrative images, and document summaries.

The system, named *Open Book*, is deployed as an editing tool for healthcare and educational service providers. It functions semi-automatically, exploiting the three processors and requiring the user to authorise the application of the conversion operations. The system is required to assess the readability of texts, not only to decide which texts should be converted, but also to assess the readability of texts that are undergoing conversion. It is expected that people working to improve the accessibility of a given text will benefit from relevant feedback concerning the effects of the changes being introduced. Automatic assessment of readability is one method by which such feedback can be delivered. In the

[6] http://www.cs.columbia.edu/ noemie/alignment/
[7] Available at: http://www.first-asd.eu/?q=system/files/FIRST_D7.2_20130228_annex.pdf
[8] www.first-asd.eu

context of improving the accessibility of texts, relevant feedback should indicate the extent to which different versions of a text meet the particular requirements of intended readers.

User requirements were obtained through consulatation of 94 subjects meeting the strict DSM-IV criteria for ASD and with IQ > 70. 43 user requirements were derived and assigned a reference code. The requirements link linguistic phenomena to editing operations, such as deletion, explanation, or transformation, that will convert the text to a more accessible form. The linguistic phenomena of concern include instances of syntactic complexity such as long sentences containing more than 15 words (possibly containing multiple copulative coordinated clauses (UR301), subordinate adjective clauses (UR302), explicative clauses (UR303), non-initial adverbial clauses (UR307)), sentences containing passive verbs (UR313), rarely used conjunctions and antithetic conjuncts (UR304, UR305, UR306), uncommon synonyms of polysemic words (UR401, UR425, UR504, UR505, UR511), rarely-used symbols and punctuation marks (UR311), anaphors, words containing more than 7 characters, adjectives ending with *-ly*, long numerical expressions (UR417), negation (UR314), words more than 7 characters long and adverbs with suffix *-ly* (UR317-319), anaphors, including pronouns (UR418-420).

Additional linguistic phenomena such as phraseological units (UR402, UR410, UR425, UR507), and non-lexicalised metaphors (UR422, UR508), were also found to pose obstacles to reading comprehension for people with ASD. At present, there is a scarcity of resources enabling accurate detection of these items. For this reason, changes in the prevalence of these items in original and converted versions of texts are not captured in this study. The full set of user requirements is detailed in Martos et al. (2013). More generally, it is infrequent linguistic phenomena that cause the greatest difficulty.

3 Related Work

There have been several studies analysing the existing TS corpora. However, their main focus was on determining necessary transformations in TS: for children (Bautista et al., 2011); for people with intellectual disability (Drndarević and Saggion, 2012); for language learners (Petersen and Ostendorf, 2007); and for people with low literacy (Gasperin et al., 2009). Unfortunately, those studies are not directly comparable (neither among themselves nor with our study), either because they focus on different types of transformations (the study of Bautista et al. (2011) focuses on general transformations while the other three studies focus on sentence transformations), or because they treat different languages (Spanish, English, and Brazilian Portuguese).

Two previous studies most relevant to ours are those by Napoles and Dredze (2010), and by Štajner et al. (2013). Napoles and Dredze (2010) built a statistical classification system that discriminates *simple* English from *ordinary* English, based on EW–SEW corpus. They used four different groups of features: lexical, part-of-speech, surface, and syntactic parse features. The accuracy of the best classifier (SVM) on the document classification task when using all features was 99.90%, while the accuracy of the best classifier (maximum entropy) on the sentence classification task when using all features was 80.80%. However, this study only demonstrated that it is fairly easy to discriminate sentences and documents of EW from those of SEW. It did not investigate whether the *simple* English used in SEW complies with the user requirements of any specific population with reading difficulties. Štajner et al. (2013) analysed a corpus of 37 newswire texts in Spanish and their manual simplifications aimed at people with Down's syndrome, compiled in the Simplext project[9]. They built a classification system that discriminates the original texts from those which are simple with an F-measure of 1.00 using the SVM, and only seven features: average number of punctuation marks (not counting end of sentence markers), numerical expressions, average word length in characters, the ratio of simple and complex sentences, sentence complexity index, lexical density and lexical richness. They reported the average sentence length as being the feature with the best discriminative power, leading to an F-measure of 0.99 when used on its own.

In spite of the many linguistic phenomena that pose obstacles to reading comprehension for different target populations, there have been almost no studies investigating whether a TS system built with a specific target population in mind could be successfully applied – or adapted – to a different target

[9]www.simplext.es

Corpus	Aimed at	Version	Code	Texts	SentPerText	WordsPerText
Weekly Reader	Language learners	Original	Learn.-O	100	39.41 ± 14.43	746.83 ± 174.25
		Simple	Learn.-S	100	38.40±12.59	621.11 ± 157.17
Enc. Britannica	Children	Original	Brit.-O	20	27.10 ± 8.91	628.30 ± 198.19
		Simple	Brit.-S	20	26.45 ± 9.35	382.35 ± 127.69
Wikipedia	Various	Original	Wiki-O	110	34.55 ± 1.87	716.57 ± 117.82
		Simple	Wiki-S	110	34.49 ± 1.82	675.07 ± 107.03
FIRST	People with ASD	Original	FIRST-O	25	13.64 ± 3.95	285.68 ± 34.46
		Simple	FIRST-S	25	22.92 ± 4.79	311.36 ± 76.82

Table 1: Corpora characteristics

population. The only exception to this is the study by Štajner and Saggion (2013), which demonstrated that two classifiers – one which discriminates sentences which should be split from those which should be left unsplit, and another which discriminates sentences which should be deleted from those which should be preserved – can successfully be trained on one type of corpora and applied to the other. Both corpora consisted of texts in Spanish, one containing newswire texts manually simplified for people with Down's syndrome, and the other various text genres manually simplified for people with ASD.

Motivated by those previous studies and the lack of parallel corpora aimed specifically to people with ASD, in this paper, we investigate whether some of already existing corpora for TS in English could potentially be used for building a data-driven TS system for this target population.

4 Methodology

The corpora, features, and experimental settings used in this study are described in Sections 4.1–4.3.

4.1 Corpora

Four parallel corpora of original and manually simplified texts for different target populations were used in this study (Table 1):

1. The corpus of 100 texts from *Weekly Reader* and their manual simplifications provided by Macmillan English Campus and Onestopenglish[10] aimed at foreign language learners. The corpus is divided into three sub-corpora – advanced, intermediate and elementary – each representing a different level of simplification. Given that the other three corpora used in this study contain original texts and only one level of simplification, we only used the texts from the advanced (henceforth *original*) and elementary (henceforth *simplified*) levels. A more detailed description of this corpus can be found in (Allen, 2009).

2. The corpus of 20 texts from the Encyclopedia Britannica and their manually simplified versions aimed at children – Britannica Elementary (Barzilay and Elhadad, 2003)[11].

3. The corpus of 110 randomly selected corresponding articles from EW and SEW. Here, it is important to note that, in general, articles from SEW do not represent direct simplifications of the articles from EW, they just have a matching topic. For this reason, we did not use complete EW and SEW articles. We only used those sentences in original and simplified versions, which existed in the sentence-aligned parallel corpora version 2.0[12] (Kauchak, 2013).

4. The corpus of 25 texts on various topics manually simplified for people with autism, compiled in the FIRST project[13], for the purpose of a piloting task[14]. The texts were simplified by carers of people with ASD in accordance with specified guidelines.

[10]http://www.onestopenglish.com/
[11]http://www.cs.columbia.edu/ noemie/alignment/
[12]http://www.cs.middlebury.edu/ dkauchak/simplification/
[13]www.first-asd.eu
[14]http://www.first-asd.eu/?q=system/files/FIRST_D7.2_20130228_annex.pdf

4.2 Text Features Relevant to User Requirements

In this paper, a set of 15 text complexity measures and 4 formulae exploiting these measures was used to estimate the accessibility of the texts. These features quantify the occurrence of linguistic phenomena identified as potential obstacles to reading comprehension for people with ASD. The set of features is presented in Table 2. The set of formulae is presented in Table 3. In every case, accessible texts are expected to have smaller values of each metric.

#	Code	Linguistic feature	Explanation/relevance
1 2 3	Illative CompConj AdvConj	Illative conjunctions Comparative conjunctions Adversative conjunctions	Indicators of syntactic complexity, linking clauses. [UR304-306]
4 5 6	LongSent Semicol Passive	Long sentences Semicolons/suspension points Passive verbs	Motivated by the assumption that deriving the propositions in complex sentences is more difficult than deriving connections between related propositions expressed in simple sentences (Arya et al., 2011). [UR309-310, UR313]
7	UnPunc	Unusual punctuation	Indicates syntactic complexity, ellipsis, alternatives, and mathematical expressions [UR311]
8	Negations	Negation	The sum of adverbial and morphological negations ("Make it Simple" (Freyhoff et al., 1998), though contrary to the findings of Tattamanti (2008)) [UR314]
9	Senses	Possible senses	The sum over all tokens in the text of the total number of possible senses of each token. [UR401, UR425, UR504-505, UR511]
10	PolyW	Polysemic words	Words with two or more senses listed in WordNet. [UR401, UR425, UR504, UR505, UR511]
11	Infreq	Infrequent words	Words that are not among the 5000 most frequent words in English [UR304-306, UR401, UR425, UR504-505, UR511]
12	NumExp	Numerical expressions	Numbers written as sequences of words rather than digits [UR417]
13 14	Pron DefDescr	Pronouns Definite descriptions	Studies have shown that people with ASD can have difficulty processing anaphora (Fine et al., 1994) [UR418-420]
15	SylLongW	Long words	Words with more than three syllables [UR317-319]

Table 2: Complexity measures (1 – words such as *therefore* and *hence*; 2 – words such as *equally* and *correspondingly*; 3 – words such as *although* and *conversely*; 4 – sentences more than 15 words long; 8 – negative adverbials and negative prefixes such as *un-* and *dis-*; 11 – derived from Wiktionary frequency lists for English[16])

#	Code	Metric	Formula	Relevance
16	PolyType	Polysemic type ratio	$\frac{ptyp}{typ}$	Indicates the proportion of the text vocabulary that is polysemous. [UR401, UR425, UR504-505, UR511]
17	CommaInd	Comma index	$\frac{10\times c}{w}$	Indicates the average syntactic complexity of the sentences in the text [UR301-303, UR307]
18	WordsPerSent	Words per sentence	$\frac{w}{s}$	Indicates the average length of the sentences in the text [UR309]
19	TypeTokRat	Type-token ratio	$\frac{typ}{tok}$	Indicate the range of vocabulary used in the text [UR401, UR425, UR504, UR505, UR511]

Table 3: Text complexity formulae (w – the number of words in the text; s – the number of sentences in the text; $ptyp$ – the number of polysemic word types in the text; c – the number of commas in the text; typ – the number of word types in the text; tok – the number of word tokens in the text)

Scores for these measures, and the text complexity formulae that exploit them where obtained automatically by the tokeniser, part-of-speech tagger, and lemmatiser distributed with LT TTT2 (Grover et al., 2000). Detection of the features used to derive complexity measures also involved the use of additional resources such as WordNet, gazetteers of rare illative, comparative, and adversative conjunctions, negatives (words and prefixes) and a set of lexico-syntactic patterns used to detect passive verbs (presented in Figure 1).

am/are/is/was/were w_{RB}* $w_{\{VBN\|VBD\}}$
am/are/is/was/were w_{RB}* *being* w_{RB}* $w_{\{VBN\|VBD\}}$
have/has/had w_{RB}* *been* w_{RB}* $w_{\{VBN\|VBD\}}$
will w_{RB}* *be* w_{RB}* $w_{\{VBN\|VBD\}}$
am/is/are w_{RB}* *going* w_{RB}* *to* w_{RB}* *be* w_{RB}* $w_{\{VBN\|VBD\}}$
w_{MD} w_{RB}* *be* $w_{\{VBN\|VBD\}}$
w_{MD} w_{RB}* *have* w_{RB}* *been* w_{RB}* $w_{\{VBN\|VBD\}}$

Figure 1: Lexico-syntactic patterns used to detect passive verbs ('*' indicates zero or more repetitions of the item it is attached to, while RB, VBN, VBD, and MD are Penn treebank tags returned by the LT TTT PoS tagger: RB – adverb; VBN – past participle; VBD – past tense; and MD – modal verb)

4.3 Experiments

Two sets of experiments were performed in this study:

1. Analysis of differences between original and simplified texts in terms of nineteen selected features (Section 4.2) across four corpora (Section 4.1). Statistical difference was measured using the t-test for related samples in the cases where the features were normally distributed, and using the related samples Wilcoxon signed rank test otherwise. Normality of the data was tested using the Shapiro-Wilk test of normality, which is preferred over the Kolmogorov-Smirnov test when the dataset contains less than 2,000 elements. All tests were performed in SPSS. Features 1–15 were first normalised (as an average per sentence) in order to allow a fair comparison across the four TS corpora (text length in words and sentences differed significantly across different corpora).

2. Classification experiments with the aim of discriminating original from simplified texts using the nineteen selected features. All experiments were conducted using the Weka Experimenter (Witten and Frank, 2005; Hall et al., 2009) in 10-fold cross-validation setup with 10 repetitions, using four different classification algorithms: NB – NaiveBayes (John and Langley, 1995), SMO – Weka implementation of Support Vector Machines (Keerthi et al., 2001) with normalisation, JRip – a propositional rule learner (Cohen, 1995), and J48 – Weka implementation of C4.5 (Quinlan, 1993). The statistical significance of the observed differences in F-measures obtained by different algorithms was calculated using the corrected paired t-test provided in the Weka Experimenter.

The TS system in FIRST is not only supposed to decide which texts should be converted, but also to assess the readability of texts that are undergoing conversion. It is expected that people working to improve the accessibility of a given text will benefit from relevant feedback concerning the effects of the changes being introduced. Automatic assessment of readability is one method by which such feedback can be delivered. Deriving a subset of features which, when trained with an appropriate classification algorithm, can categorize a given text as either 'original' or 'simplified', would facilitate automatic evaluation of TS systems. The resulting classifier would be suitable for assessing whether those systems perform an appropriate level of simplification. This could serve as a rough estimation, an efficient first step offering a quick evaluation prior to being tested with real users.

5 Results and Discussion

The results of the two sets of experiments are presented and discussed in the next two subsections.

5.1 Analysis of the Features across the Corpora

Mean values (with standard deviations) of each of the first eight features on each sub-corpus are displayed in Table 4. The number of unusual punctuation marks (*UnPunc*) is the only feature whose value does not differ significantly between the original and simplified versions of the texts in any of the four corpora. This feature was thus excluded from further classification experiments. The number of comparative conjunctions per sentence (*CompConj*) significantly decreases only when simplifying texts for

Corpus	Illative	CompConj	AdvConj	LongSent	Semicol	UnPunc	Passive	Negations
Lear.-O	0.24±0.12	0.04±0.13	0.21±0.08	0.62±0.15	0.03±0.05	0.00±0.01	0.21±0.10	0.33±0.15
Lear.-S	**0.20±0.13**	0.03±0.09	**0.19±0.09**	**0.51±0.14**	***0.03±0.05**	0.00±0.01	**0.09±0.09**	**0.26±0.14**
Brit.-O	0.13±0.09	0.15±0.26	0.14±0.07	0.72±0.11	0.13±0.20	0±0	0.33±0.10	0.28±0.16
Brit.-S	**0.08±0.05**	***0.02±0.10**	**0.06±0.04**	**0.38±0.11**	**0.00±0.02**	0±0	**0.25±0.12**	**0.14±0.09**
Wiki-O	0.20±0.11	0.11±0.19	0.16±0.10	0.65±0.12	0.04±0.04	0.04±0.10	0.34±0.15	0.32±0.23
Wiki-S	**0.18±0.11**	0.11±0.20	**0.14±0.09**	**0.62±0.12**	**0.03±0.04**	0.03±0.10	0.33±0.15	**0.29±0.24**
FIRST-O	0.18±0.14	0.06±0.19	0.18±0.15	0.68±0.15	0.03±0.10	0.01±0.02	0.27±0.23	0.42±0.28
FIRST-S	**0.11±0.10**	0.01±0.06	**0.09±0.07**	**0.33±0.19**	0.00±0.01	0±0	0.20±0.15	**0.22±0.13**

Table 4: Mean values (with standard deviation) of features 1–8 across the corpora (*O* – the original texts in the corpora; *S* – the simplified texts in the corpora; **bold** – significantly different from the value on the original texts at a 0.01 level of significance; ***bold** – significantly different from the value on the original texts at a 0.05 level of significance (but not at 0.01); '0.00' – a value different from zero which rounded at two decimals gives 0.00; '0' – a value equal to zero)

Corpus	Senses	PolyW	Infreq	NumExp	Pron	DefDescr	SylLongW
Lear.-O	73.95±12.32	9.37±1.72	5.64±1.33	0.18±0.11	0.97±0.40	1.86±0.54	1.12±0.28
Lear.-S	**64.21±11.16**	**7.85±1.45**	**4.14±1.01**	**0.16±0.10**	**0.90±0.37**	**1.62±0.45**	**0.92±0.27**
Brit.-O	67.51± 8.83	9.87±1.15	9.37±1.10	0.18±0.12	0.40±0.18	2.86±0.44	1.45±0.20
Brit.-S	**48.68± 4.17**	**6.48±0.57**	**5.39±0.58**	**0.09±0.06**	**0.28±0.13**	**1.86±0.20**	**1.17±0.19**
Wiki-O	67.70±12.96	9.13±1.61	7.86±1.63	0.18±0.16	0.67±0.43	2.08±0.58	1.24±0.38
Wiki-S	68.20±13.56	**8.71±1.56**	**7.16±1.51**	***0.17±0.16**	0.68±0.44	**1.97±0.54**	**1.10±0.42**
FIRST-O	82.28±24.20	10.16±2.65	7.11±2.72	0.19±0.19	1.05±0.73	2.12±0.92	1.17±0.58
FIRST-S	**57.13±15.96**	**6.47±1.77**	**3.92±1.56**	**0.09±0.07**	***0.82±0.44**	**1.62±0.54**	***0.92±0.43**

Table 5: Mean values (with standard deviation) of features 9–15 across the corpora (*O* – the original texts in the corpora; *S* – the simplified texts in the corpora; **bold** – significantly different from the value on the original texts at a 0.01 level of significance; ***bold** – significantly different from the value on the original texts at a 0.05 level of significance (but not at 0.01))

children (*Brit.-S*), while the average number of passive constructions per sentence (*Passive*) decreases when simplifying for both children (*Brit.-S*) and language learners (*Lear.-S*). It is interesting to note that the average number of passive constructions per sentence (*Passive*) does not decrease in the EW–SEW corpus and that its value on the simplified versions of Wikipedia articles (*Wiki-S*) is significantly higher than on *Brit.-S* and *Lear.-S*, although SEW claims to provide articles simplified for both those target populations. It can also be observed that the fact that all four corpora were reported to have significant differences between original and simplified texts in terms of features *Illative*, *AdvConj*, *LongSent*, and *Negations* does not necessarily mean that the average number of occurrences of those features is similar in all four simplified corpora. The values of *Illative*, *AdvConj*, and *LongSent* in the simplified versions of the texts in the FIRST corpus seem to correspond best to those in the simplified versions of the texts in the Britannica corpus (*Brit.-S*). The value of *Negations* in *FIRST-S*, however, seems to correspond best to that in *Lear.-S*. This suggests that if we wish to build a component of our TS system (to assist people with ASD) which would remove negations (*Negations*), we should train it on the sentence pairs from the corpora with simplifications aimed at second language learners. If we wish to build a component which would remove illative conjunctions (*Illative*), adversative conjuctions (*AdvConj*), or long sentences (*LongSent*), we should probably train it on the sentence pairs from the corpora with simplifications aimed at young readers.

The number of occurrences per sentence of features 9–15 in the original versions of the texts was significantly higher than in the simplified versions of the texts in all four corpora, with only two exceptions – features *Senses* and *Pron* in the EW–SEW corpus (*Wiki-O* and *Wiki-S*), as can be observed in Table 5. Again, the mean values of all features in the simplified versions of the texts in the FIRST corpora *FIRST-S*, seems to correspond better to the simplified versions of Encyclopedia Britannica (*Brit.-S*) and

Corpus	PolyType	CommaInd	WordsPerSent	TypeTokRat
Lear.-O	0.76±0.04	0.56±0.12	19.91±3.46	0.51±0.04
Lear.-S	**0.77±0.04**	**0.46±0.15**	**16.69±2.78**	**0.47±0.05**
Brit.-O	0.69±0.03	0.78±0.15	23.46±2.78	0.51±0.04
Brit.-S	***0.71±0.02**	***0.67±0.14**	**14.61±1.21**	**0.55±0.04**
Wiki-O	0.71±0.05	0.65±0.15	20.73±3.16	0.48±0.05
Wiki-S	**0.71±0.05**	**0.60±0.16**	**19.57±2.90**	***0.48±0.05**
FIRST-O	0.73±0.04	0.51±0.18	22.20±5.43	0.59±0.05
FIRST-S	0.75±0.06	**0.19±0.15**	**13.86±3.41**	**0.53±0.08**

Table 6: Mean values (with standard deviation) of features 16–19 across the corpora (*O* – the original texts in the corpora; *S* – the simplified texts in the corpora; **bold** and ***bold** – used in the same way as in the previous two tables)

Weekly Readers (*Lear.-S*) than to those in the simplified versions of the Wikipedia articles (*Wiki-S*). It is also interesting to note that many of the features (*LongSent*, *Negations*, *Senses*, *PolyW*, *Infreq*, *DefDesc*) seem to have a significantly higher number of occurrences per sentence in the simplified versions of the Wikipedia articles (*Wiki-S*) than in the simplified versions of Encyclopedia Britannica (*Brit.-S*) and Weekly Reader (*Lear.-S*).

The comma index (*CommaInd*), type-token ratio (*TypeTokRat*), and the average number of words per sentence (*WordsPerSent*) were found to be significantly higher in original texts than in their simplified versions in all four corpora (Table 6). However, the values of those three text complexity formulae were not similar in the simplified texts across the four corpora. In terms of the average number of words per sentence (*WordsPerSent*) and the type-token ratio (*TypeTokRat*), the simplified versions of the texts in the FIRST corpora (*FIRST-S*) seem to correspond better to the texts simplified for young readers (*Brit.-S*), than to those simplified for second language learners (*Lear.-S*) and those aimed at various target populations (*Brit.-S*). The comma index (*CommaInd*) obtained for simplified texts in the FIRST corpora was several times lower than that obtained for simplified texts in the three other corpora. The polysemic type ratio (*PolyType*) was not significantly different in original and in simplified texts of the FIRST corpora (Table 6). The higher polysemic type ratio (*PolyType*) for simplified rather than original versions of the texts in the other three corpora was unexpected, as it is usually assumed that polysemous words can pose an obstacle for various target populations. However, it is important to bear in mind that polysemous words usually pose an obstacle when conveying one of their infrequently used meanings. Findings in cognitive psychology indicate that the words with the highest number of possible meanings are actually understood more quickly, due to their high frequency (Jastrzembski, 1981). A common lexical simplification strategy is to replace infrequent words with their more frequent synonyms, and long words with their shorter synonyms. This strategy leads to a higher polysemic type ratio (*PolyType*) in simplified versions of the texts as the shorter words are usually more frequent (Balota et al., 2004), and frequent words tend to be more polysemous than infrequent ones (Glanzer and Bowles, 1976).

5.2 Classification between Original and Simplified Texts

Classification experiments were conducted using two different sets of features on each of the corpora:

1. *all* – all 18 features (UnPunc was excluded as it was not reported as significant for any of the corpora)
2. *best* – 11 features which were reported as significant for all four corpora (Illative, AdvConj, LongSent, Negations, PolyW, NumExp, DefDescr, SylLongW, CommaInd, WordsPerSent, TypeTokRat)

As can be observed from Table 7, use of the SMO-n classification algorithm using the subset of 11 *best* features achieves perfect 1.00 F-measure for discriminating original from simplified versions of the Encyclopedia Britannica. The same classification algorithm performs less well on the FIRST and Weekly Readers corpora (though still quite well), while it performs significantly worse on the Wikipedia corpus.

The baseline (which chooses majority class) would be 0.50 in all cases. These results indicate that the Encyclopedia Britannica TS parallel corpus, and possibly the Weekly Readers TS parallel corpus, may serve as suitable training material for building a TS system (or at least some of its components) aimed at people with ASD.

Dataset	SMO-n	NB	JRip	J48
Brit-all	0.98±0.09	0.94±0.12	0.94±0.14	0.97±0.11
Brit-best	1.00±0.00	0.99±0.05	0.94±0.13	0.97±0.11
FIRST-all	0.88±0.15	0.86±0.19	0.79±0.23	0.75±0.25
FIRST-best	0.88±0.15	0.85±0.20	0.78±0.25	0.76±0.25
Lear-all	0.81±0.08	0.74±0.10*	0.75±0.07*	0.72±0.10*
Lear-best	0.77±0.08	0.74±0.11	0.70±0.10*	0.73±0.10
Wiki-all	0.54±0.12	0.50±0.12	0.51±0.14	0.35±0.20*
Wiki-best	0.55±0.13	0.55±0.12	0.51±0.12	0.33±0.20*

Table 7: F-measure with standard deviation in a 10-fold cross-validation setup with 10 repetitions for four classification algorithms: SMO-n, NB, JRip, and J48 (* – statistically significant degradation in comparison with SMO-n)

6 Conclusions

Automatic Text Simplification (ATS) aims to convert complex texts into a simpler form, which is more accessible to a wider audience. Due to the lack of parallel corpora for TS consisting of original and manually simplified texts, most of the ATS systems for specific target populations are still rule-based. Our main goal was to explore whether some of the existing TS parallel corpora in English, aimed at different audiences (children – Encyclopedia Britannica, language learners – Weekly Reader, and various – Wikipedia) could be used as training material to build a TS system aimed at people with ASD. We analysed the four corpora (FIRST, Britannica, Weekly Reader, and Wikipedia) in terms of nineteen linguistic features which pose obstacles to reading comprehension for people with ASD. The preliminary results indicate that the Britannica TS parallel corpus, and possibly the Weekly Reader TS parallel corpus, could be used to train a TS system aimed at people with ASD. Two sets of classification experiments which tried to discriminate original from simplified texts according to the nineteen features derived from user requirements further supported those findings. The results of the classification experiments indicated that the SVM classifier trained on the Britannica corpus might be suitable for discriminating original from simplified texts for people with ASD, and thus might be used as the initial evaluation of the texts simplified by the TS system developed in the FIRST project.

Acknowledgements

The research described in this paper was partially funded by the European Commission under the Seventh (FP7-2007-2013) Framework Programme for Research and Technological Development (FP7-ICT-2011.5.5 FIRST 287607).

References

D. Allen. 2009. A Corpus-Based Study of the Role of Relative Clauses in the Simplification of News Texts for Learners of English. *System*, 37(4):585–599.

S. M. Aluísio, L. Specia, T. A.S. Pardo, E. G. Maziero, and R. P.M. Fortes. 2008. Towards brazilian portuguese automatic text simplification systems. In *Proceedings of the eighth ACM symposium on Document engineering*, DocEng '08, pages 240–248, New York, NY, USA. ACM.

D. J. Arya, Elfrieda H. Hiebert, and P. D. Pearson. 2011. The effects of syntactic and lexical complexity on the comprehension of elementary science texts. *International Electronic Journal of Elementary Education*, 4 (1):107–125.

D. Balota, M. J. Cortese, S. D. Sergent-Marshall, D. H. Spieler, and M. J. Yap. 2004. Visual word recognition of single-syllabe words. *Journal of Experimental Psychology: General*, 133:283–316.

E. Barbu, M. Martín-Valdivia, L. Alfonso, and U. Lopez. 2013. Open book: a tool for helping asd users' semantic comprehension. In *Proceedings of the 2th Workshop of Natural Language Processing for Improving Textual Accessibility (NLP4ITA)*, pages 11–19, Atlanta, US. Association for Computational Linguistics.

R. Barzilay and N. Elhadad. 2003. Sentence alignment for monolingual comparable corpora. In *Proceedings of the 2003 conference on Empirical methods in natural language processing*, EMNLP '03, pages 25–32, Stroudsburg, PA, USA. Association for Computational Linguistics.

S. Bautista, C. León, R. Hervás, and P. Gervás. 2011. Empirical identification of text simplification strategies for reading-impaired people. In *European Conference for the Advancement of Assistive Technology*.

O. Biran, S. Brody, and N. Elhadad. 2011. Putting it Simply: a Context-Aware Approach to Lexical Simplification. In *Proceedings of the 49th Annual Meeting of the Association for Computational Linguistics: Human Language Technologies*, pages 496–501, Portland, Oregon, USA. Association for Computational Linguistics.

J. Carroll, G. Minnen, Y. Canning, S. Devlin, and J. Tait. 1998. Practical Simplification of English Newspaper Text to Assist Aphasic Readers. In *Proceedings of AAAI-98 Workshop on Integrating Artificial Intelligence and Assistive Technology*, pages 7–10.

W. Cohen. 1995. Fast Effective Rule Induction. In *Proceedings of the Twelfth International Conference on Machine Learning*, pages 115–123.

W. Coster and D. Kauchak. 2011. Learning to Simplify Sentences Using Wikipedia. In *Proceedings of the 49th Annual Meeting of the Association for Computational Linguistics*, pages 1–9.

S. Devlin and G. Unthank. 2006. Helping aphasic people process online information. In *Proceedings of the 8th international ACM SIGACCESS conference on Computers and accessibility*, Assets '06, pages 225–226, New York, NY, USA. ACM.

I. Dornescu, R. Evans, and C. Orasan. 2013. A Tagging Approach to Identify Complex Constituents for Text Simplification. In *Proceedings of Recent Advances in Natural Language Processing*, pages 221 – 229, Hissar, Bulgaria.

B Drndarević and H. Saggion. 2012. Reducing Text Complexity through Automatic Lexical Simplification: an Empirical Study for Spanish. *SEPLN Journal*, 49.

R. Evans, C. Orasan, and I. Dornescu. 2014. An evaluation of syntactic simplification rules for people with autism. In *Proceedings of the 3rd Workshop on Predicting and Improving Text Readability for Target Reader Populations (PITR)*, pages 131–140, Gothenburg, Sweden, April. Association for Computational Linguistics.

J. Fine, G. Bartolucci, P. Szatmari, and G. Ginsberg. 1994. Cohesive discourse in pervasive developmental disorders. *Journal of Autism and Developmental Disorders*, 24:315–329.

G. Freyhoff, G. Hess, L. Kerr, B. Tronbacke, and K. Van Der Veken, 1998. *Make it Simple, European Guidelines for the Production of Easy-toRead Information for People with Learning Disability*. ILSMH European Association, Brussels.

C. Gasperin, L. Specia, T. Pereira, and S.M. Aluísio. 2009. Learning When to Simplify Sentences for Natural Text Simplification. In *Proceedings of the Encontro Nacional de Inteligncia Artificial (ENIA-2009), Bento Gonalves, Brazil.*, pages 809–818.

M. Glanzer and N. Bowles. 1976. Analysis of the word frequency effect in recognition memory. *Journal of Experimental Psychology: Human Learning and Memory*, 2:21–31.

C. Grover, C. Matheson, A. Mikheev, and M. Moens. 2000. Lt ttt - a flexible tokenisation tool. In *In Proceedings of Second International Conference on Language Resources and Evaluation*, pages 1147–1154.

M. Hall, E. Frank, G. Holmes, B. Pfahringer, P. Reutemann, and I. H. Witten. 2009. The weka data mining software: an update. *SIGKDD Explor. Newsl.*, 11:10–18, November.

K. Inui, A. Fujita, T. Takahashi, R. Iida, and T. Iwakura. 2003. Text simplification for reading assistance: a project note. In *Proceedings of the second international workshop on Paraphrasing - Volume 16*, PARAPHRASE '03, pages 9–16, Stroudsburg, PA, USA. Association for Computational Linguistics.

J. Jastrzembski. 1981. Multiple meaning, number or related meanings, frequency of occurrence and the lexicon. *Cognitive Psychology*, 13:278–305.

G. H. John and P. Langley. 1995. Estimating Continuous Distributions in Bayesian Classifiers. In *Proceedings of the Eleventh Conference on Uncertainty in Artificial Intelligence*, pages 338–345.

D. Kauchak. 2013. Improving text simplification language modeling using unsimplified text data. In *Proceedings of the 51st Annual Meeting of the Association for Computational Linguistics (Volume 1: Long Papers)*, pages 1537–1546, Sofia, Bulgaria, August. Association for Computational Linguistics.

S. S. Keerthi, S. K. Shevade, C. Bhattacharyya, and K. R. K. Murthy. 2001. Improvements to Platt's SMO Algorithm for SVM Classifier Design. *Neural Computation*, 13(3):637–649.

S. T. Kover, E. Haebig, A. Oakes, A. McDuffie, R. J. Hagerman, and L. Abbeduto. 2012. Syntactic comprehension in boys with autism spectrum disorders: Evidence from specific constructions. In *Proceedings of the 2012 International Meeting for Autism Research*, Athens, Greece. International Society for Autism Research.

J. Martos, S. Freire, A. González, D. Gil, R. Evans, V. Jordanova, A. Cerga, A. Shishkova, and C. Orasan. 2013. FIRST Deliverable - User preferences: Updated. Technical Report D2.2, Deletrea, Madrid, Spain.

C. Napoles and M. Dredze. 2010. Learning simple wikipedia: a cogitation in ascertaining abecedarian language. In *Proceedings of the NAACL HLT 2010 Workshop on Computational Linguistics and Writing: Writing Processes and Authoring Aids*, CL&W '10, pages 42–50, Stroudsburg, PA, USA. Association for Computational Linguistics.

S. E. Petersen and M. Ostendorf. 2007. Text Simplification for Language Learners: A Corpus Analysis. In *Proceedings of Workshop on Speech and Language Technology for Education*.

R. Quinlan. 1993. *C4.5: Programs for Machine Learning*. Morgan Kaufmann Publishers, San Mateo, CA.

H. Saggion, E. Gómez Martínez, E. Etayo, A. Anula, and L. Bourg. 2011. Text Simplification in Simplext: Making Text More Accessible. *Revista de la Sociedad Española para el Procesamiento del Lenguaje Natural*, 47:341–342.

H. Tager-Flusberg. 1981. Sentence comprehension in autistic children. *Applied Psycholinguistics*, 2:1:5–24.

M. Tattamanti, R. Manenti, P. A. Della Rosa, A. Falini, D. Perani, S. Cappa, and A. Moro. 2008. Negation in the brain: Modulating action representations. *NeuroImage*, 43 (2008):358–367.

UN. 2006. Convention on the rigths of persons with disabilities.

F. R. Volkmar and L. Wiesner. 2009. *A Practical Guide to Autism*. Wiley, Hoboken, NJ, 2nd edition.

S. Štajner and H. Saggion. 2013. Adapting Text Simplification Decisions to Different Text Genres and Target Users. *Procesamiento del Lenguaje Natural*, 51:135–142.

S. Štajner, B. Drndarević, and H. Saggion. 2013. Corpus-based Sentence Deletion and Split Decisions for Spanish Text Simplification. *Computación y Systemas*, 17(2):251–262.

I. H. Witten and E. Frank. 2005. *Data mining: practical machine learning tools and techniques*. Morgan Kaufmann Publishers.

K. Woodsend and M. Lapata. 2011. Learning to Simplify Sentences with Quasi-Synchronous Grammar and Integer Programming. In *Proceedings of the 2011 Conference on Empirical Methods in Natural Language Processing (EMNLP)*.

S. Wubben, A. van den Bosch, and E. Krahmer. 2012. Sentence simplification by monolingual machine translation. In *Proceedings of the 50th Annual Meeting of the Association for Computational Linguistics: Long Papers - Volume 1*, ACL '12, pages 1015–1024, Stroudsburg, PA, USA. Association for Computational Linguistics.

M. Yatskar, B. Pang, C. Danescu-Niculescu-Mizil, and L. Lee. 2010. For the sake of simplicity: unsupervised extraction of lexical simplifications from wikipedia. In *Human Language Technologies: The 2010 Annual Conference of the North American Chapter of the Association for Computational Linguistics*, HLT '10, pages 365–368, Stroudsburg, PA, USA. Association for Computational Linguistics.

Z. Zhu, D. Berndard, and I. Gurevych. 2010. A Monolingual Tree-based Translation Model for Sentence Simplification. In *Proceedings of the 23rd International Conference on Computational Linguistics (Coling 2010)*, pages 1353–1361.

Making historical texts accessible to everybody

Cristina Vertan
University of Hamburg
Vogt-Kölln Strasse 30
22529 Hamburg
cristina.vertan@uni-hamburg.de

Walther v. Hahn
University of Hamburg
Vogt-Kölln Strasse 30
22529 Hamburg
vhahn@informatik.uni-hamburg.de

Abstract

In this paper we discuss the degree of readability of historical texts for a broad public. We argue that text simplification methods can improve significantly this aspect and bring an added value to historical texts. We present a specific example, a genuine multilingual historical texts, which should be available at least to researchers from different fields and propose a mechanism for simplifying the text.

1 Introduction

During the last decade there was a massive digitization campaign, which lead to a large number of electronicly available collections of historical documents. Most of these collections offer the possibility to navigate through the documents and display not only the associated metadata but also content. Thus researchers and students in various fields, which are related to one document's topic, may have access to it.

This, however, is not a barrier-free access as many historical languages either differ significantly from their modern correspondent or they are not at all in use any longer.

Thus only scholars can understand such texts with deep knowledge in the respective language(s). We use the plural form „languages" as most historical texts are multilingual, being composed from a mixture of paragraphs in one main text language and one or e more secondary languages which were either linguae francae at the time when the document has been written (e.g. Latin, Ancient Greek, Arabic) or reflect cultural or geographical particularities of the topic being described (e.g. a Latin Document written about the organisation of the Turkish empire).

Text simplification is a technique used up to now for making modern texts accessible to groups with special requirements (persons with disabilities, language learners). Simplification means a broad range of techniques from lexical replacements of less used terms by more frequent ones, through syntactic adaptation (substitution of relative clauses, elimination of long distance dependencies) up to reshaping on the discourse level (e.g. eliminating anaphora) (Saggion et. al. 2013), (Dornescu et. al. 2013). However, it is assumed that the users know orthography and morphology of the language.

In this paper we argue that text simplification is also an adequate method for making historical texts understandable for a broader public and we describe first approaches with a genuine multilingual historical text. The paper is organised as follows: in section 2 we introduce simplification requirements for historical texts and exemplify them by means of a particular scenario, which we will describe. Section 3 is dedicated to our approach towards text simplification. Finally in section 4 we present our first conclusions and further work to be done.

2 The Need of Text Simplification for historical Texts

As we mentioned in section 1, historical texts must suffer a certain transformation in order to be understood by non-trained readers. These transformations are language dependent and should satisfy two criteria:

- They should try to bring the text as close as possible to the modern language form (if available)
- They should preserve the cultural and geographical setting of the time when they were written.

In the following paragraph we will consider texts (originals or historical translations) for which a modern variant of the language is still in use.

As an example we will discuss the works of Dimitrie Cantemir, political figure, philosopher, historian, musician, geographer, who lived at the end of XVIIth. century and prepared two important works for the history of Eastern Europe for the Royal Academy of Sciences in Berlin. The first one, „Decriptio Moldaviae“ (The Description of Moldavia) is - as the title suggests - a detailed presentation of his (Cantemir's) native country Moldavia (spreading today from the eastern part of Romania to the current Republic of Moldavia). Cantemir describes the history of the country, as well as its geography, the language and the traditions of people living there. It includes also the first detailed map of the region. The work was written in Latin and translated into German and French at the beginning of the XVIIIth century, later into Romanian. The second work is „The History of Growth and Decay of the Ottoman Empire“. This was again written in Latin and translated more or less immediately into German, French, English and Russian. It remained a reference work for studies of the Ottoman Empire until the middle of XIXth century.

Both works are thus relevant for historians but also for ethnographers, linguists, as well as for people interested in the history of these three territories.

The fact that they were translated seems to make their reception easier. However we will show through several examples that this is a false assumption. The following examples illustrate also the need of text simplification at four linguistic levels: orthography morphology, syntax and semantics.

The following examples are extracted from the German translation from 1771 of "Descriptio Moldaviae" (Cantemir 1771). They are, however illustrative for a wide range of historical texts in other language combinations. A more detailed description can be found in XXXXXXXX

2.1 2.1. Orthographic level

In this text we encounter passages in German, Romanian, Latin and Ancient Greek. German Text is written in black-letter typeface. Latin and part of Romanian words (see below) are written with roman typeface. Greek paragraphs are easyly to detect and to isolate due to their specific alphabet.

Two approaches of the writer were identified when dealing with local (Romanian) names

- Named Entities (geographical names, person names) as well as names for specific roles in the army or society are written with black-letter typeface. They are adapted to the German pronunciation, like in the following examples:

  e.g. The river Prut became Pruth; The ruler Dragoș became Dragosch, the role of being a „pivnicier“ (person responsible for keeping wine and goods in the basement of a castle) became „pivnichar“

- Lexical items illustrating the language, remained in Latin font and were not adapted phonetically. However, as at Cantemir's time Romanian language was written in Cyrillic alphabet, the Latin-alphabet transcription is deviant from the current Romanian orthography

  e.g. "*muiere*" (colloquial term for woman) appears in text as "*mujere*".

2.2 Morphological and syntactic level

Old morphological forms deviant from those used in current German are present throughout the book

e.g. „*zweyten*" or „*Theil*" instead of "*zweiten*" and "*Teil*"

For any modern reader unknown named entities appear: e.g. *„in dem bergigten Theile von Moramor, (*)"*. Even in the text the *„Moramor"* region is not clearly identified and the text passage contains two footnotes "(*)", one from Cantemir himself and one from the German translator from 1771, both commenting the word *Moramor*.

2.3 Semantic level

There are either words which still exist in the modern vocabulary but mostly used with a different meaning. An example is the word *„flüchtigen"* used in the XVIIIth century exclusively with the meaning of *„running away from somebody"* whereas nowadays it is predominantly used with the meaning of *„volatile substance"*. The main challenge here is that both meanings were and are still valid through the whole period from XVIIIth century until now, just the usage frequency of one or the other meaning changed.

Time references are often relative. In an expression like *„von dem heutigen Ungarn"* (engl. *„from Hungary nowadays"*) one should understand and interpret the temporal expression „nowadays" as referring to the time when the text was written (even not: published). This also implies that the corresponding political or geographical unit, in this case *„Hungary"* may have changed since that time.

2.4 Knowledge level

Additionally at knowledge level one can observe a different conceptual representation. We present here just one relevant example: It refers to geographical units / population groups, which changed their denomination or may refer to different entities depending of the historical/geographical context. In the sentence

> *„Die auf der andern Seite angränzende Polen und Russen nennen die Moldauer Wolochen, d. i.* ***Wälsche*** *oder Italiäner, die Walachen aber, die auf dem Gebirge wohnen, heissen sie die Berg-Walachen, oder die Leute jenseits des Gebirges*

we find the term ***„Wälsche"***. In Central Germany up to the last century *„Wälsche"* was the name for French, in Southern Germany for Italians and still today in Eastern Austria it is the name for Slovenians. Thus the term depends on the historical and geographical context and is not fixed to a specific population. However, readers may be confused without this background knowledge.

From the examples above it is clear that a non-trained reader (i.e. a reader being not familiar with Early New High German, Romanian and old terms in Romanian, Romanian geography and history) will have difficulties in reading and interpreting the text. We should mention here that there does not exist any modern German Edition of the text.

3 Text simplification for historical texts

We argue that a process of text simplification should take place at all above-mentioned levels. Some parts (the orthographical and morphological/syntactical level can be done semi-automatically through a rule-based process. Prerequisite is that the text is digitized and the information concerning the typeface and the font is preserved.

- STEP 1: Within the black-letter typeface paragraphs
  - Match each word against a German language model,
  - If a word is not matched but there are candidates from which it differs by 1 or 2 words try to apply normalization rules like (ey → ei, ev → eu),
  - In contrary match the word against a Romanian language model and try the same with a set of Romanian normalization rules. Words which could not be matched should be rendered to the user and proposed for manual correction.
- STEP 2: Within the Latin-typeface phrases
  - Match words against a Latin language model and a Romanian one

- Word which could be found in both should be rendered for manual annotation and language disambiguation,
- For words not found in the Latin model but with some close variants in the Romanian language model try to apply a Romanian normalization rule.

The output of Steps 1 and 2 will be a normalized text in with language is identified and marked for all paragraphs.

The paragraphs marked by "Romanian" have to be manually translated, i.e. explained to the reader in German or English.

Additional annotation is necessary to enable text processing for text simplification at upper levels. We propose an annotation scheme, aiming not only at marking words which could not be corrected throughout the normalization process, but enhancing also the meaning of the word (Vertan and v. Hahn 2014)

The main unit of the annotation is called „phrase". By phrase we mean a word or a multi-word expression. For each phrase the semantic frame includes information about the named entity (if any) as well as the obsolete meaning and the modern meaning of the word.

In figure 1 we present the structure of the annotation, while in figure 2 we present an example of an annotation as well as the possible linkage to a domain ontology

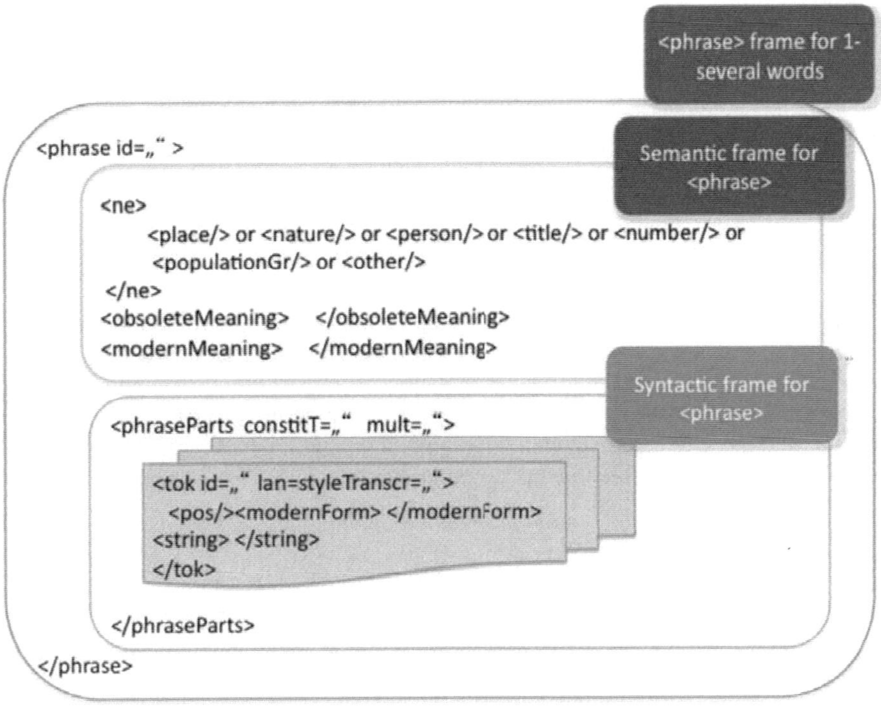

Figure 1 Structure of the annotation scheme

Following this annotation step, a replacement of each annotated phrase with its modern form or in case of Romanian or Latin words with its translation will be obtained. Our first attempts in applying a rule-based constraint dependency parser (Beuck et. al. 2011) on such text were successful but this needs deeper investigation. The dependency parser can be used for identifying relative clauses and proposes candidates for further simplification.

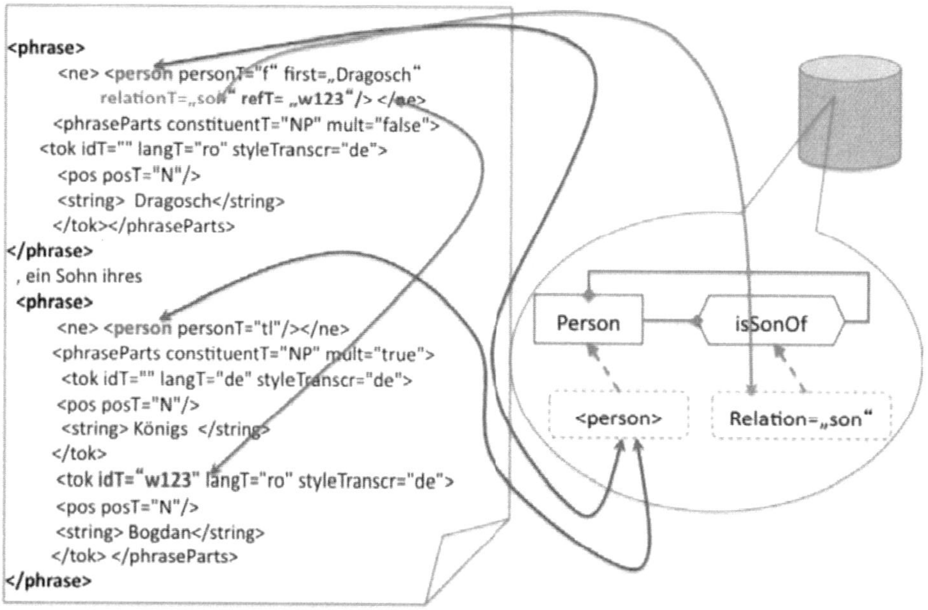

Figure 2 Example of annotation scheme and ontology linking

4 Conclusions and further work

In this paper we showed that text simplification is a useful technique for making historical texts understandable for modern readers. We identified particularities of historical texts, which need special attention and pre-processing. In the second step we are able to apply state-of-the-art methods for text simplification. We propose an algorithm dealing with multilingual entries for text normalization.

Currently we are annotating manually the words rendered by the normalization process. Further work is planned for the application of the WCDG parser on the normalized text and selection of relative clauses, which can be either deleted or transformed into a main clause, in order to make sentences shorter and clearer. We intend also to exploit the existence of a comparable corpus containing translations of the same text in five languages (Vertan 2014).

References

Niels Beuck, Arne Köhn, and Wolfgang Menzel. Incremental parsing and the evaluation of partial dependency analyses In DepLing 2011, Proceedings of the 1st International Conference on Dependency Linguistics, 2011.

Cantemir Dimitire Beschreibung der Moldau. *Faksimildruck der Original Ausgabe von 1771, Maciuca C. (Ed).* , Bukarest, Kriterion Verlag, 1973

Iustin Dornescu, Richard Evans and Constantin Orasan, A tagging Approach to Identify Complex Constitutents for Text Simplification, in Proceedings of Recent Advances in Natural Language Processing (RANLP 2013), Hisar, Bulgaria, pp.221-229

Horacio Saggion, Elena Gomez-Martinez, Alberto Anula, Lorena Bourg, Esteban Etayo, Text Simplification in Simplext: Making texts more Accessible, last retrieved at www.simplext.es

Cristina Vertan and Walther v. Hahn, Discovering and Explaining Knowledge in historical Documents, Proceedings of the Workshop on "Language Technology for Historical Languages and Newspaper Archives", Kristin Bjnadottir, Stewen Krauwer, Cristina Vertan and Martin Wyne Eds., Workshop associated with LREC 2014, Rejkyavik Mai 2014, pages 76-79

Cristina Vertan, Less explored multilingual issues in the automatic processing of historical texts – a case study, Proceedings of the Digital Humanites Conference 2014, Lausanne, pages 406-407